Math Contests
for
Grades 4, 5, and 6
Volume 3

School Years
1991-92 through 1995-96

Written by

Steven R. Conrad • Daniel Flegler

Published by MATH LEAGUE PRESS
Printed in the United States of America

Cover art by Bob DeRosa

Phil Frank Cartoons Copyright © 1993 by CMS

First Printing, 1996

Copyright © 1996
by Mathematics Leagues Inc.
All Rights Reserved

Math League Press
P.O. Box 720
Tenafly, NJ 07670-0720

ISBN 0-940805-09-X

Preface

Math Contests—Grades 4, 5, and 6, Volume 3 is the third volume in our series of problem books for grades 4, 5, and 6. The first two volumes contain the contests given in the school years 1979-80 through 1990-91. This volume contains contests given from 1991-92 through 1995-96. (You can use the order form on page 154 to order any of our 9 books.)

This book is divided into three sections for ease of use by students and teachers. You'll find the contests in the first section. Each contest consists of 30 or 40 multiple-choice questions that you can do in 30 minutes. On each 3-page contest, the questions on the 1st page are generally straightforward, those on the 2nd page are moderate in difficulty, and those on the 3rd page are more difficult. In the second section of the book, you'll find detailed solutions to all the contest questions. In the third and final section of the book are the letter answers to each contest. In this section, you'll also find rating scales you can use to rate your performance.

Many people prefer to consult the answer section rather than the solution section when first reviewing a contest. We believe that reworking a problem when you know the answer (but *not* the solution) often leads to increased understanding of problem-solving techniques.

Each year we sponsor an Annual 4th Grade Mathematics Contest, an Annual 5th Grade Mathematics Contest, and an Annual 6th Grade Mathematics Contest. A student may participate in the contest on grade level or for any higher grade level. For example, students in grades 4 and 5 (or below) may participate in the 6th Grade Contest. Starting with the 1991-92 school year, students have been permitted to use calculators on any of our contests.

Steven R. Conrad & Daniel Flegler, contest authors

Acknowledgments

For her continued patience and understanding, special thanks to Marina Conrad, whose only mathematical skill, an important one, is the ability to count the ways.

For her lifelong support and encouragement, special thanks to Mildred Flegler.

To Mark Motyka, we offer our gratitude for his assistance over the years.

To Brian and Keith Conrad, who did an awesome proofreading job, thanks!

Table Of Contents

The Contests

· ·

1991-92 through 1995-96

4th Grade Contests

1991-92 through 1995-96

1991-92 Annual 4th Grade Contest

Spring, 1992

Instructions

4

- **Time** You will have only *30 minutes* working time for this contest. You might be *unable* to finish all 30 questions in the time allowed.

- **Scores** Please remember that *this is a contest, not a test*—and there is no "passing" or "failing" score. Few students score as high as 24 points (80% correct). Students with half that, 12 points, *deserve commendation!*

- **Format and Point Value** This is a multiple-choice contest. Each answer is an A, B, C, or D. Write each answer in the *Answer Column* to the right of each question. A correct answer is worth 1 point. Unanswered questions get no credit. You **may** use a calculator.

Copyright © 1992 by Mathematics Leagues Inc.

1. $0 + 0 + 0 + 0 + 0 + 0 + 0 + 0 + 0 + 0 + 0 =$

   A) 0 B) 1 C) 10 D) 11

   1.

2. Five years ago, I was 5 years old. Five years from now, I will be ? years old.

   A) 10 B) 15 C) 20 D) 25

   2.

3. $1 + 2 + 3 + 4 = 11 + 12 + 13 + 14 - \underline{?}$

   A) 10 B) 15 C) 40 D) 50

   3.

4. Ten-thousand divided by two-thousand equals

   A) 5 B) 20 C) 5000 D) 8000

   4.

5. $2 + 2 + 2 + 2 =$

   A) 2 B) 2×2 C) $2 \times 2 \times 2$ D) $2 \times 2 \times 2 \times 2$

   5.

6. What is the remainder when 7778 is divided by 7?

   A) 0 B) 1 C) 2 D) 8

   6.

7. $30 \times 40 = 3 \times 4 \times \underline{?}$.

   A) 0 B) 10 C) 100 D) 400

   7.

8. Which of the following sums is an odd number?

   A) $51 + 51$ B) $36 + 63$ C) $12 + 24$ D) $49 + 51$

   8.

9. If I have three dozen pens, then I have ? pens.

   A) 30 B) 36 C) 39 D) 42

   9.

10. $1 \times 9 \times 9 \times 2 =$

    A) 21 B) 162 C) 180 D) 1992

    10.

11. How many whole numbers are less than 1000?

    A) 997 B) 998 C) 999 D) 1000

    11.

12. If today is Monday, then 14 days from today will be

    A) Monday B) Tuesday C) Friday D) Sunday

    12.

Go on to the next page ▐▐▐▶ **4**

13. In the list of numbers 1, 2, 3, 4, 5, 6, 7, 8, 9, how many of the numbers in the list are exactly 2 more than some other number in the list?

A) 2 B) 7 C) 9 D) 11

13.

14. If bubble gum costs 5¢ per piece, the number of pieces that Ali can buy for $2.00 is

A) 10 B) 20 C) 40 D) 195

14.

15. What number must I multiply by 3 to get a product of 51?

A) 153 B) 27 C) 17 D) 16

15.

16. $(1993 - 1992) \div (1992 - 1991) =$

A) 0 B) 1 C) 1991 D) 1992

16.

17. John is 3 cm taller than Jim and 2 cm shorter than Jill. Jill is _?_ than Jim.

A) 5 cm taller B) 5 cm shorter
C) 1 cm taller D) 1 cm shorter

17.

18. If Eric and Anna have been best friends for six and one-half years, they have been best friends for _?_ months.

A) 65 B) 68 C) 72 D) 78

18.

19. On a sheet of paper, a line is drawn through the center C of a square. How many times does this line intersect (cross) the square?

·C

A) 0 B) 1 C) 2 D) 3

19.

20. Of the following, which is the largest product?

A) 47×53 B) 48×52 C) 49×51 D) 50×50

20.

21. What is the time 16 minutes *before* 3:15 P.M.?

A) 2:59 P.M. B) 2:99 P.M. C) 3:59 P.M. D) 4:59 P.M.

21.

22. 1234 + 5678 =

A) 6666 B) 6789 C) 6912 D) 7032

22.

Go on to the next page ⫸ **4**

23. I am going to retire when I am 65 years old. How old am I now if I am going to retire in 30 years?

A) 20   B) 25   C) 30   D) 35

23.

24. If special stamps cost 17¢ each, how much does it cost to buy 8 of these special stamps?

A) 25¢   B) 56¢   C) $1.26   D) $1.36

24.

25. (50 – 40) + (40 – 30) + (30 – 20) + (20 – 10) =

A) 50   B) 50 – 10   C) 50 + 10   D) 50 × 10

25.

26. What is the tens' digit of the *largest* 4-digit even number which uses each of the digits 5, 7, 8, and 9 exactly once?

A) 9   B) 8   C) 7   D) 5

26.

27. When a certain number is divided by 3, the quotient is 240. When that same number is divided by 6, the quotient is

A) 720   B) 480   C) 120   D) 80

27.

28. The Incredible Shrinking Boy becomes 4 cm shorter each year. If he is 2 m tall when he is 10 years old, how tall will he be when he is 25 years old?

A) 140 cm   B) 100 cm   C) 60 cm   D) 40 cm

28.

29. The product of 1000 whole numbers is 1000. What is the *largest* possible value the sum of these numbers can have?

A) 1000   B) 1992   C) 1993   D) 1999

29.

30. Square *ABCD* is divided into four smaller squares, as shown in the diagram. The perimeter of each of the four smaller squares is 4. What is the perimeter of square *ABCD*?

A) 8   B) 12   C) 16   D) 20

30.

The end of the contest ✍ **4**

Solutions on Page 73 • Answers on Page 138

1992-93 Annual 4th Grade Contest

Spring, 1993

Instructions

4

- **Time** You will have only *30 minutes* working time for this contest. You might be *unable* to finish all 30 questions in the time allowed.

- **Scores** Please remember that *this is a contest, not a test*—and there is no "passing" or "failing" score. Few students score as high as 24 points (80% correct). Students with half that, 12 points, *deserve commendation!*

- **Format and Point Value** This is a multiple-choice contest. Each answer is an A, B, C, or D. Write each answer in the *Answer Column* to the right of each question. A correct answer is worth 1 point. Unanswered questions get no credit. You **may** use a calculator.

1. $2 + 4 + 6 + 8 = 1 + 3 + 5 + 7 +$?

   A) 0 　　　　 B) 1 　　　　 C) 4 　　　　 D) 9

   1.

2. The sum of the thousands' digit and the tens' digit of 12345 is

   A) 5 　　　　 B) 6 　　　　 C) 7 　　　　 D) 8

   2.

3. $(12 \times 7) - (12 + 12 + 12 + 12) =$

   A) 36 　　　 B) 48 　　　 C) 72 　　　 D) 108

   3.

4. The product of the number of sides of a rectangle and the number of sides of a triangle is

   A) 9 　　　　 B) 12 　　　 C) 16 　　　 D) 20

   4.

5. $9 + 9 + 9 + 9 + 9 + 9 + 9 = 9 \times$?

   A) 6 　　　　 B) 7 　　　　 C) 8 　　　　 D) 9

   5.

6. The number 1 million is less than the number

   A) 1 thousand 　　　　 B) 10 thousand
   C) 100 thousand 　　　 D) 1 billion

   6.

7. I had 3 dozen socks in my drawer, but I lost 2 pairs. How many socks do I now have in my drawer?

   A) 32 　　　 B) 34 　　　 C) 36 　　　 D) 40

   7.

8. $1 + 10 + 100 + 1000 =$

   A) 4 　　　 B) 1111 　　　 C) 1234 　　　 D) 4000

   8.

9. If the wool from 1 sheep can make 4 sweaters, how many sheep are needed to make 100 sweaters?

   A) 4 　　　　 B) 5 　　　　 C) 25 　　　 D) 400

   9.

10. Which of the following products is odd?

    A) 30×9 　 B) 3×90 　 C) 30×90 　 D) 3×9

    10.

11. The number of months in a year minus the number of days in a week equals

    A) 5 　　　　 B) 7 　　　　 C) 9 　　　　 D) 19

    11.

12. $5 + 50 + 500 = 5 \times$?

    A) 10 　　　 B) 100 　　　 C) 111 　　　 D) 550

    12.

Go on to the next page ⇒ **4**

13. For a quarter (25¢), Pat can play a video game for 5 minutes. How many quarters does Pat need to play for an hour?

    A) 10   B) 12   C) 20   D) 55

13.

14. Which of the following is *not* equal to 10?

    A) $100 \div 10$ B) $10 \div 1$ C) 10×1 D) 100×10

14.

15. If 1 Earth year is equal to 3 years on the planet Trizone, how many Earth years are equal to 12 years on the planet Trizone?

    A) 4   B) 10   C) 36   D) 48

15.

16. What time is it 58 minutes before 6:10 P.M.?

    A) 5:08 P.M.   B) 5:12 P.M.   C) 7:08 P.M.   D) 7:12 P.M.

16.

17. Otto the octopus needs 2 tentacles to juggle up to 3 balls. If Otto uses all 8 tentacles, Otto can juggle up to _?_ balls.

    A) 8   B) 9   C) 12   D) 24

17.

18. How many days are there in *exactly* 52 weeks?

    A) 364   B) 365   C) 366   D) 367

18.

19. $99 + 99 + 99 + 101 + 101 + 101 =$

    A) 200   B) 300   C) 600   D) 919

19.

20. If today is Tuesday, what day was it 76 days ago?

    A) Monday   B) Tuesday   C) Wednesday   D) Thursday

20.

21. The lengths of three sides of a rectangle are 1992, 1993, and 1993. What is the length of the fourth side of this rectangle?

    A) 1992   B) 1993   C) 1994   D) 1995

21.

22. $40 \times 50 \times 60 = 4 \times 5 \times 6 \times \underline{\ ?\ }$

    A) 10   B) 100   C) 456   D) 1000

22.

23. 94 is 49 more than

    A) 45   B) 50   C) 54   D) 55

23.

Go on to the next page ⫸ **4**

		Answer Column

24. Scrooge told his secretary to double his yearly gift to the Bulldogs. His secretary said that his gift would still be the same amount after doubling. What is Scrooge's yearly gift?

A) $0   B) $1   C) $10   D) $100

24.

25. How many more hours are there in a leap year than in a year which is not a leap year?

A) 1   B) 24   C) 48   D) 366

25.

26. Seventy-seven hundred is equal to

A) 70×70 B) 7×7000 C) 7×110 D) 11×700

26.

27. What is the *largest* number which is both less than $2 \times 3 \times 5 \times 7$ *and* also a divisor of $2 \times 3 \times 5 \times 7$?

A) 357   B) 2357   C) $2 \times 5 \times 7$ D) $3 \times 5 \times 7$

27.

28. A *prime* number is a number greater than 1 whose only whole number factors are itself and 1. What is the smallest *prime* number greater than 50?

A) 51   B) 52   C) 53   D) 59

28.

29. A bag contains 2 red, 2 blue, and 2 green marbles. Sue takes one marble at a time from this bag without looking. What is the least number of marbles Sue must take from this bag to be *sure* that she has taken 2 marbles of the same color?

A) 2   B) 3   C) 4   D) 6

29.

30. A square sheet of paper is cut along a straight line into two pieces. Neither of these two pieces can be a

A) pentagon   B) triangle   C) rectangle   D) square

30.

The end of the contest ✍ **4**

Solutions on Page 77 • Answers on Page 139

12

1993-94 Annual 4th Grade Contest

Spring, 1994

Instructions

4

- **Time** You will have only *30 minutes* working time for this contest. You might be *unable* to finish all 30 questions in the time allowed.

- **Scores** Please remember that *this is a contest, not a test*—and there is no "passing" or "failing" score. Few students score as high as 24 points (80% correct). Students with half that, 12 points, *deserve commendation!*

- **Format and Point Value** This is a multiple-choice contest. Each answer is an A, B, C, or D. Write each answer in the *Answer Column* to the right of each question. A correct answer is worth 1 point. Unanswered questions get no credit. You **may** use a calculator.

1. $1 \times 9 \times 9 \times 4 =$

    A) 23   B) 36   C) 324   D) 1994

1.

2. What is 2 more than 4 more than 6?

    A) 14   B) 12   C) 10   D) 8

2.

3. $77 - 66 + 55 - 44 + 33 - 22 + 11 = 11 + \underline{?}$

    A) 0   B) 11   C) 22   D) 33

3.

4. Jim has 1 dozen *pairs* of socks. How many socks does Jim have?

    A) 6   B) 14   C) 24   D) 144

4.

5. What number is 999 more than 111?

    A) 1000   B) 1010   C) 1110   D) 1111

5.

6. If I multiply 13 by 13 and divide the result by 13, I get $\underline{?}$

    A) 169   B) 13   C) 1   D) 0

6.

7. If today is Monday, then 2 days before yesterday was

    A) Saturday   B) Sunday   C) Thursday   D) Friday

7.

8. $(1 + 2 + 3 + 4 + 5 + 6) - (1 + 3 + 5) = \underline{?}$

    A) 8   B) 12   C) 21   D) 248

8.

9. Of the following sums, which one is *not* equal to $20 + 20 + 20$?

    A) $14 + 20 + 24$ B) $19 + 20 + 21$
    C) $10 + 20 + 30$ D) $0 + 20 + 40$

9.

10. $100 \times 0 \times 10 \times 0 \times 1 \times 0 = \underline{?}$

    A) 0   B) 111   C) 100 101   D) 1 000 000

10.

11. Wilt watches the weather in Waterville. He noticed that, in 1993, it rained on 1 of every 3 cloudy days in Waterville. If it rained on 36 days in Waterville in 1993, how many cloudy days were there in Waterville in 1993?

    A) 12   B) 39   C) 72   D) 108

11.

12. $22 \times 22 = 11 \times 11 \times \underline{?}$

    A) 2   B) 4   C) 11   D) 121

12.

Go on to the next page ▐▉▶ **4**

14

13. I have 1 quarter, 1 dime, and 3 nickels. These 5 coins are worth the same amount as ? pennies.

A) 5   B) 40   C) 50   D) 113

13.

14. A sentence is a *palindrome* if it reads the same forwards or backwards when we ignore both punctuation and capitalization. For example, the sentence "Was it a rat I saw?" is a palindrome. How many of the following sentences are palindromes?
   I. Gateman sees names, garageman sees name tag.
   II. A man, a plan, a canal—Panama!
   III. Tini saw drawer and reward was in it.
   IV. Ma is as selfless as I am.

A) 1   B) 2   C) 3   D) 4

14.

15. $10 + 10 + 10 = 20 + 20 + 20 -$?

A) 3   B) 10   C) 20   D) 30

15.

16. (The number of sides a rectangle has) + (the number of sides a square has) − (the number of sides a triangle has) =

A) 4   B) 5   C) 7   D) 11

16.

17. $77 + 77 + 77 = 21 \times$?

A) 6   B) 7   C) 11   D) 14

17.

18. It takes Genie 20 minutes to teach his dog Moe to sit, 35 minutes to teach Moe to lie down, and 40 minutes to teach Moe to roll over. If Genie started to teach Moe all three tricks at 1:40 P.M. and worked without stopping, at what time was Genie finished?

A) 2:15 P.M.   B) 2:35 P.M.   C) 3:15 P.M.   D) 3:35 P.M.

18.

19. Of the following, which number is divisible by 11 and 111?

A) 111   B) 1111   C) 11 111   D) 111 111

19.

20. (11 hundreds) + (11 tens) + (11 ones) =

A) 1111   B) 1221   C) 11 110   D) 12 210

20.

21. What is the smallest whole number greater then 42 which is divisible by 6?

A) 43   B) 45   C) 46   D) 48

21.

Go on to the next page ⫸ **4**

22. While signing a book, Lee used all the letters of the alphabet that came after *b* but before *y*. If Lee used no other letters, how many different letters did Lee use?

    A) 21   B) 22   C) 23   D) 24

22.

23. What is the remainder when 1 234 567 is divided by 10?

    A) 7   B) 5   C) 3   D) 1

23.

24. If the length of a diameter of a circle is 10, what is the length of a radius of this circle?

    A) 5   B) 10   C) 15   D) 20

24.

25. The sum of the ages of Sam, Sara, and Sue is 26. What will be the sum of their ages in four years?

    A) 30   B) 33   C) 34   D) 38

25.

26. Al has 5 quarters. Bob has only dimes and pennies, but the value of Bob's coins is the same as the value of Al's coins. What is the *smallest* number of coins Bob can have?

    A) 13   B) 15   C) 17   D) 25

26.

27. If I add 1994 to any odd number, the sum will *always* be

    A) odd   B) even   C) 1995   D) prime

27.

28. The roller coaster in my town gives rides to 16 people every 3 minutes. The ferris wheel gives rides to 9 people every 2 minutes. In 6 minutes, how many more people can ride the roller coaster than can ride the ferris wheel?

    A) 5   B) 14   C) 21   D) 30

28.

29. In diagram I, there are 3 different rectangles: 2 small rectangles and 1 large rectangle. How many different rectangles are there in diagram II?

    A) 4   B) 5   C) 7   D) 10

29.

30. If $2 + 4 + 6 + \ldots + 198 + 200 = 10\,100$, what is the value of $1 + 3 + 5 + \ldots + 197 + 199$?

    A) 5050   B) 9900   C) 10 000   D) 10 099

30.

The end of the contest 🖐 **4**

Solutions on Page 81 • Answers on Page 140

16

1994-95 Annual 4th Grade Contest

Spring, 1995

Instructions

4

- **Time** You will have only *30 minutes* working time for this contest. You might be *unable* to finish all 30 questions in the time allowed.

- **Scores** Please remember that *this is a contest, not a test*—and there is no "passing" or "failing" score. Few students score as high as 24 points (80% correct). Students with half that, 12 points, *deserve commendation!*

- **Format and Point Value** This is a multiple-choice contest. Each answer is an A, B, C, or D. Write each answer in the *Answer Column* to the right of each question. A correct answer is worth 1 point. Unanswered questions get no credit. You **may** use a calculator.

1. How many 1's must be added to $1 + 1 + 1$ for the total to be 8?

   A) 1   B) 3   C) 5   D) 8

   1.

2. The number of letters in the alphabet plus the number of days in a week equals

   A) 31   B) 32   C) 33   D) 182

   2.

3. $1 \times 1995 \times 1 =$

   A) 405   B) 1995   C) 1997   D) 2996

   3.

4. The remainder when $5+5+5+5+5+5+5+5$ is divided by 4 is

   A) 0   B) 1   C) 3   D) 10

   4.

5. Which of the following is not a factor of 420?

   A) 5   B) 6   C) 7   D) 8

   5.

6. If a bobsled can seat 7 kids, how many kids can be seated on 77 bobsleds?

   A) 11   B) 84   C) 539   D) 777

   6.

7. $2 \times 2 \times 2 \times 2 = 1 \times 1 \times 1 \times 1 \times \underline{?}$

   A) 2   B) 4   C) 8   D) 16

   7.

8. Add the hundreds' digit of 321 to the product of the tens' digit of 987 and the ones' digit of 654. The sum should be

   A) 32   B) 35   C) 64   D) 96

   8.

9. $(1994 + 1995 + 1996) - (1993 + 1994 + 1995) =$

   A) 1   B) 3   C) 6   D) 1996

   9.

10. In a family of 60 mice, each mouse eats 2 kg of cheese every 30 days. How much cheese does this family eat every day?

    A) 4 kg   B) 3 kg   C) 2 kg   D) 1 kg

    10.

11. If 1 decade is 10 years, then 100 decades is $\underline{?}$ years.

    A) 10   B) 100   C) 110   D) 1000

    11.

12. The sum of all even numbers bigger than 2 and smaller than 12 is

    A) 14   B) 26   C) 28   D) 30

    12.

Go on to the next page ▐▶ **4**

18

13. $7 \times 1 \times 1 \times 1 \times 1 \times 1 \times 1 \times 1 \times 7 =$

    A) 717   B) 49   C) 21   D) 7

13.

14. Of the following, which could *not* be the difference between an even number and an odd number?

    A) 1   B) 9   C) 32   D) 77

14.

15. Five less than six more than seven ears of corn is ? ears of corn.

    A) 6   B) 7   C) 8   D) 9

15.

16. 38 hours after 11 o'clock is ? o'clock.

    A) 1   B) 2   C) 8   D) 12

16.

17. Rita's rabbit hops twice as far as Larry's leapfrog. The rabbit jumps 2 m with each hop. If both pets take 3 hops in the same direction, how much further does the rabbit go than the frog?

    A) 1 m   B) 2 m   C) 3 m   D) 6 m

17.

18. $4 + 4 + 4 + 4 + 4 + 4 =$? $\times (2 + 2 + 2)$

    A) 2   B) 4   C) 6   D) 8

18.

19. In the garden of Lenny the Leprechaun, only one 4-leaf clover grows for every ten 3-leaf clovers that grow. How many leaves are there in Lenny's garden of 22 clovers?

    A) 66   B) 68   C) 88   D) 154

19.

20. The product of the first three prime numbers is

    A) 6   B) 24   C) 30   D) 42

20.

21. A square has the same number of sides as a

    A) trapezoid   B) pentagon   C) triangle   D) hexagon

21.

22. Tarzan rode his elephant from 5:45 PM to 7:15 PM. For how many minutes did Tarzan ride his elephant that day?

    A) 170   B) 150

    C) 120   D) 90

22.

Go on to the next page IIII➡ **4**

23. I divide $1\times2\times3\times4\times5\times6\times7$ by a certain whole number. Then I divide the quotient by the same whole number. I continue dividing each new quotient by the same whole number until the remainder is no longer 0. By which of the following whole numbers can I divide the largest number of times?

    A) 2   B) 3   C) 4   D) 5

    23.

24. A 99¢ ticket is worth how many more nickels than a 24¢ ticket?

    A) 13   B) 15   C) 25   D) 75

    24.

25. A whole number that has exactly two factors must be

    A) even   B) odd   C) prime   D) more than 2

    25.

26. I multiply a whole number by itself. The ones' digit of this product *cannot* be

    A) 0   B) 5   C) 6   D) 7

    26.

27. I started listing the odd whole numbers in order. My list began: 1, 3, 5, ... If the last number I listed was 1995 and I did not skip any number, how many numbers were on my list?

    A) 997   B) 998   C) 999   D) 1995

    27.

28. A month is called a *prime* month if the total number of days in the month is a prime number. How many *prime* months are there in 1995?

    A) 0   B) 5   C) 6   D) 7

    28.

29. Captain Quark can run the Intergalactic Marathon twice as fast as Mr. Spoke. If Mr. Spoke can run it in 7 hours and 10 minutes, then Captain Quark can run it in

    A) 3 hr 5 min   B) 3 hr 35 min
    C) 3 hr 55 min   D) 14 hr 20 min

    29.

30. The difference between two whole numbers is 2. The sum of the two integers may be

    A) 1995   B) 1997   C) 1999   D) 2000

    30.

The end of the contest **4**

Solutions on Page 85 • Answers on Page 141

20

1995-96 Annual 4th Grade Contest

Spring, 1996

Instructions

4

- **Time** You will have only *30 minutes* working time for this contest. You might be *unable* to finish all 30 questions in the time allowed.

- **Scores** Please remember that *this is a contest, not a test*—and there is no "passing" or "failing" score. Few students score as high as 24 points (80% correct). Students with half that, 12 points, *deserve commendation!*

- **Format and Point Value** This is a multiple-choice contest. Each answer is an A, B, C, or D. Write each answer in the *Answer Column* to the right of each question. A correct answer is worth 1 point. Unanswered questions get no credit. You **may** use a calculator.

1. 1+1 + 1+1 + 1+1 + 1+1 + 1+1 =

   A) 5×2 B) 4×2 C) 2×2 D) 1×2

   1.

2. 1999 − 1996 is the same as 99 − ?

   A) 3   B) 6   C) 19   D) 96

   2.

3. 99 + 111 = 200 + ?

   A) 0   B) 10   C) 11   D) 20

   3.

4. Which of the following divisions has the smallest remainder?

   A) $4002 \div 4$ B) $503 \div 5$ C) $604 \div 6$ D) $75 \div 7$

   4.

5. Halfway up a hill, my friends and I stopped to pick berries. We picked 76 blackberries, 54 raspberries, 32 strawberries, and 1 gigantic blueberry. How many berries did we pick altogether?

   A) 153   B) 161   C) 163   D) 165

   5.

6. $(100 \div 10) \div 10$ =

   A) 0   B) 1   C) 10   D) 80

   6.

7. $1\times3\times1\times3\times1\times3$ =

   A) 3   B) 9   C) 12   D) 27

   7.

8. In the word ? , there are as many vowels as consonants.

   A) add   B) subtract   C) multiply   D) divide

   8.

9. A crow earned a nickel for each hour it sang. If it earned 70¢ singing, how many hours did the crow sing?

   A) 7   B) 12   C) 14   D) 35

   9.

10. The product of three fives equals

    A) 125   B) 50   C) 25   D) 15

    10.

11. Two dozen pairs of pears is ? pears.

    A) 12   B) 24   C) 40   D) 48

    11.

12. If today is a Tuesday, then 15 days ago was a

    A) Saturday   B) Sunday   C) Monday   D) Wednesday

    12.

Go on to the next page ▶ **4**

13. How many odd numbers are there between 20 and 30?

    A) 4   B) 5   C) 9   D) 10

13.

14. Alice is only 30 cm tall. If eating all her veggies will make her 5 times as tall, Alice will grow to ? cm by eating all her veggies.

    A) 6   B) 35   C) 50   D) 150

14.

15. $(77 + 77 + 77) \div 7 = 66 \div$?

    A) 2   B) 3   C) 6   D) 11

15.

16. What is the ones' digit of $(100 \times 9) + (20 \times 9) + (3 \times 9)$?

    A) 0   B) 7   C) 8   D) 9

16.

17. If I counted 40 legs in a herd of sheep, how many sheep are in the herd?

    A) 10   B) 20
    C) 36   D) 160

17.

18. Monday I skated 1 km. Each day, I skate twice as far as the day before. When will I first skate more than 20 km in a day?

    A) Friday   B) Saturday   C) Sunday   D) Monday

18.

19. Every letter appeared 3 times in Di's alphabet soup. Di used some letters to spell the word "cholesterol." Using the remaining letters, she could *not* have spelled the word

    A) "add"   B) "subtract"
    C) "multiply" D) "divide"

19.

20. $1 \times 4 \times 16 = 2 \times 8 \times$?

    A) 1   B) 2   C) 4   D) 8

20.

21. A *Mega* comic costs 3 times as much as a *Multi* comic. If one *Mega* comic costs 15¢ more than two *Multi* comics, how much does one *Mega* comic cost?

    A) 5¢   B) 10¢   C) 30¢   D) 45¢

21.

Go on to the next page ⫸ **4**

23

22. Dale arrived at a party 35 minutes before 2:22 P.M. What time was it 18 minutes after Dale arrived?

    A) 1:29 P.M.   B) 1:47 P.M.   C) 2:05 P.M.   D) 2:40 P.M.

22.

23. The admission fee for the Carnival is $4 per person. If I had $26, I could pay this admission fee for myself and at most _?_ friends.

    A) 4   B) 5   C) 6   D) 7

23.

24. If Mr. Sixpence counted to 600 by 6's, starting with 6, he counted _?_ numbers that are less than 600.

    A) 98   B) 99   C) 100   D) 101

24.

25. If the length of each side of a rectangle is an odd number, then the perimeter of the rectangle could be

    A) 15   B) 17   C) 19   D) 20

25.

26. How many triangles are in the figure at the right?

    A) 5   B) 9   C) 10   D) 15

26.

27. Of the following, which number is most nearly doubled when the order of its digits is reversed?

    A) 1002   B) 2003   C) 4668   D) 6003

27.

28. If my chicken lays 5 eggs each week, how many weeks would it take her to lay 15 dozen eggs?

    A) 18   B) 36   C) 60   D) 180

28.

29. $10+20+30+40 = (1+2+3+4) \times$ _?_

    A) 10   B) 40   C) 100   D) 10 000

29.

30. What is the ones' digit of $0 + 1 + 2 + 3 + \ldots + 97 + 98$, the sum of the first 99 whole numbers?

    A) 9   B) 5   C) 1   D) 0

30.

The end of the contest ✍ **4**

Solutions on Page 89 • Answers on Page 142

5th Grade Contests

. . . .

1991-92 through 1995-96

1991-92 Annual 5th Grade Contest

Spring, 1992

Instructions

5

- **Time** Do *not* open this booklet until you are told by your teacher to begin. You will have only *30 minutes* working time for this contest. You might be *unable* to finish all 30 questions in the time allowed.

- **Scores** Please remember that *this is a contest, not a test*—and there is no "passing" or "failing" score. Few students score as high as 24 points (80% correct). Students with half that, 12 points, *should be commended!*

- **Format and Point Value** This is a multiple-choice contest. Each answer is an A, B, C, or D. Write each answer in the *Answer Column* to the right of each question. A correct answer is worth 1 point. Unanswered questions get no credit. You **may** use a calculator.

1. $(1992 + 1992) \times (1992 - 1992) =$

   A) 0   B) 1   C) 1992   D) 3984

   1.

2. Each of the following sums is less than 100 *except*

   A) 47 + 48   B) 50 + 51   C) 49 + 50   D) 48 + 49

   2.

3. $703 + 307 =$

   A) 110   B) 1010   C) 1100   D) 10010

   3.

4. What is the product of the number of days in a week and the number of months in a year?

   A) 5   B) 19   C) 60   D) 84

   4.

5. $(11 + 22 + 33) \div (1 + 2 + 3) =$

   A) 10   B) 11   C) 30   D) 33

   5.

6. Which of the following numbers has the *most* whole number factors?

   A) 4   B) 5   C) 8   D) 9

   6.

7. Jack has seven dozen pencils and Jill has eight dozen pencils. How many more pencils does Jill have than Jack?

   A) 1   B) 12   C) 24   D) 96

   7.

8. Each of the following sums is an even number *except*

   A) 977 + 111   B) 282 + 828   C) 189 + 891   D) 949 + 494

   8.

9. The sum of 7 numbers is 567. Their average is

   A) 81   B) 88   C) 91   D) 98

   9.

10. $1 + 2 + 3 + 4 + 5 = 11 + 12 + 13 + 14 + 15 - \underline{?}$

    A) 10   B) 16   C) 50   D) 100

    10.

11. In what month does the 100th day of the year occur?

    A) March   B) April   C) May   D) June

    11.

Go on to the next page ⫸ **5**

12. $1 \times 2 \times 3 \times 4 \times 5 \times 6 = 2 \times 12 \times \underline{\;?\;}$

A) 18   B) 20   C) 24   D) 30

12.

13. Which of the following numbers leaves a remainder of 1 when divided by 4?

A) 37   B) 35   C) 31   D) 27

13.

14. $1 + 22 + 333 + 4444 =$

A) 4790   B) 4800   C) 5000   D) 5100

14.

15. I own 1 white, 2 black, and 3 brown pigs. If all of these pigs could talk, how many of them could truthfully say "I am the same color as one or more of the other pigs."

A) 3   B) 4   C) 5   D) 6

15.

16. If Chip and Dale have been good friends for nine and one-half years, they have been good friends for $\underline{\;?\;}$ months.

A) 95   B) 104   C) 108   D) 114

16.

17. The number 1992 has 4 digits. How many digits does the product $10 \times 10 \times 10 \times 10 \times 10 \times 10$ have, after it is simplified?

A) 6   B) 7   C) 10   D) 1 000 000

17.

18. Of the following, which *cannot* be the number of points in which a line can intersect (cross or touch) a circle?

A) 3   B) 2   C) 1   D) 0

18.

19. Ann *makes* 5 out of every 6 shots she tries when she plays basketball. Out of 30 shots Ann tries, she will *make* $\underline{\;?\;}$ shots.

A) 20   B) 24   C) 25   D) 29

19.

20. Which of the following products is equal to 1 million?

A) 10×10 B) 100×100 C) 1000×100 D) 1000×1000

20.

21. Michael must be in school by 8 A.M. If Michael leaves his home at 7:21 A.M., he has $\underline{\;?\;}$ minutes to get to school on time.

A) 21   B) 29   C) 39   D) 79

21.

Go on to the next page IIII➡ **5**

22. Which of the following numbers is divisible by 15?

    A) 115   B) 215   C) 315   D) 415

    22.

23. The sum of two consecutive whole numbers is 1993. What is the difference between these two numbers?

    A) 1   B) 2   C) 996   D) 1992

    23.

24. If two different whole numbers are both less than 10, their product *could* equal

    A) 0   B) 1   C) 100   D) 101

    24.

25. $(27 \times 31 \times 35 \times 39 \times 43) \div (43 \times 39 \times 35 \times 31) =$

    A) 1   B) 4   C) 5   D) 27

    25.

26. The smallest odd number greater than 399 is divided by 10. The remainder of this division is

    A) 0   B) 1   C) 3   D) 9

    26.

27. In rectangle *ABCD*, which of the following line segments is parallel to $\overline{BD}$?

    A) $\overline{AB}$ B) $\overline{CD}$ C) $\overline{BC}$ D) $\overline{AC}$

    27.

28. Every prime between 30 and 100 has a ones' digit that is

    A) 1   B) 3   C) odd   D) even

    28.

29. If 5 gizmos = 3 gremlins, then 45 gremlins = _?_ gizmos.

    A) 27   B) 30   C) 47   D) 75

    29.

30. A whole number is a *perfect square* if it can be expressed as the product of two equal whole numbers. For example, 9 is a perfect square since $9 = 3 \times 3$. How many perfect squares are greater than 0 and less than 1000?

    A) 30   B) 31   C) 32   D) 33

    30.

The end of the contest ✍ **5**

Solutions on Page 95 • Answers on Page 143

1992-93 Annual 5th Grade Contest

Spring, 1993

Instructions

5

- **Time** Do *not* open this booklet until you are told by your teacher to begin. You will have only *30 minutes* working time for this contest. You might be *unable* to finish all 30 questions in the time allowed.

- **Scores** Please remember that *this is a contest, not a test*—and there is no "passing" or "failing" score. Few students score as high as 24 points (80% correct). Students with half that, 12 points, *should be commended!*

- **Format and Point Value** This is a multiple-choice contest. Each answer is an A, B, C, or D. Write each answer in the *Answer Column* to the right of each question. A correct answer is worth 1 point. Unanswered questions get no credit. You **may** use a calculator.

Answer
Column

1. $11 + 12 + 13 = 10 + 11 + 12 + \underline{?}$

   A) 0   B) 1   C) 3   D) 6

1.

2. 8 hundreds + 17 tens =

   A) 8170   B) 870   C) 817   D) 970

2.

3. Six people stand in a circle, each with 4 pears. After each person passes 2 pears to the person on the right, each person will have

   A) 2 pears   B) 4 pears   C) 6 pears   D) 12 pears

3.

4. $32 \div 2 = 2 \times \underline{?}$

   A) 4   B) 8   C) 16   D) 32

4.

5. A certain bird flies south. If it flies 120 km each day and it flies 3000 km in all, how many days does it take to make the trip?

   A) 120   B) 50   C) 25   D) 15

5.

6. $(1 \times 2 \times 3 \times 4 \times 5) \div 10 =$

   A) 7   B) 12   C) 23   D) 24

6.

7. The difference between two numbers is 333. If the smaller number is 321, the larger number is

   A) 666   B) 654   C) 456   D) 345

7.

8. $10 + 100 + 1000 = 10 \times \underline{?}$

   A) 100   B) 110   C) 111   D) 1000

8.

9. Which of the following quotients is an odd number?

   A) $128 \div 128$ B) $128 \div 64$ C) $128 \div 32$ D) $128 \div 16$

9.

10. (Number of sides of a square) + (number of sides of a pentagon) − (number of sides of a hexagon) = number of sides of _?_

   A) a triangle   B) a rectangle   C) a pentagon   D) an octagon

10.

11. $(7 \times 15) - (7 + 14 + 21 + 28) = 7 \times \underline{?}$

   A) 0   B) 1   C) 3   D) 5

11.

12. Mary can buy 5 candy bars for 60¢. How much would it cost her for 10 candy bars?

   A) 12¢   B) 65¢   C) $1.20   D) $3.00

12.

Go on to the next page ⅢⅢ➡ **5**

13. The average of 7, 7, 7, 7, 7, 7, and 21 is

    A) 7   B) 8   C) 9   D) 14

13.

14. The product 303×11 is the 4-digit number 3333. The product $2 \times 2 \times 2 \times 2 \times 2 \times 2 \times 5 \times 5 \times 5 \times 5 \times 5 \times 5$ is a _?_ -digit number.

    A) 6   B) 7   C) 10   D) 12

14.

15. What is the sum of the ten-thousands' digit and the hundreds' digit of 1 234 567?

    A) 6   B) 7   C) 8   D) 9

15.

16. 341 is 143 more than

    A) 198   B) 208   C) 218   D) 484

16.

17. What is the *remainder* when 1 414 146 is divided by 7?

    A) 0   B) 1   C) 2   D) 6

17.

18. Of the following, which is most nearly equal to $1?

    A) 96 pennies   B) 17 nickels   C) 12 dimes   D) 5 quarters

18.

19. What is the time 2 hours and 57 minutes *before* 12:10 A.M.?

    A) 9:13 P.M.   B) 10:07 P.M.   C) 10:13 P.M.   D) 3:07 A.M.

19.

20. $10 \times 20 \times 30 = 6 \times$ _?_

    A) 10   B) 100   C) 500   D) 1000

20.

21. As shown, *ABCD* is a rectangle. Which of the following is a pair of parallel sides?

    A) $\overline{AB}, \overline{BC}$ B) $\overline{DA}, \overline{AB}$ C) $\overline{AB}, \overline{CD}$ D) $\overline{DC}, \overline{BC}$

21.

22. I am thinking of two numbers. The first number is 30 less than twice the second number. If the second number is 16, what is the sum of these two numbers?

    A) 2   B) 18   C) 46   D) 48

22.

23. A polygon *cannot* have _?_ sides.

    A) 2   B) 3   C) 7   D) 1993

23.

Go on to the next page ➠ **5**

24. The average of my three test grades is 60. If I get 100 on my next test, my average will then be

    A) 80   B) 75   C) 70   D) 65

25. What is the ones' digit of the product 37 × 37 × 37?

    A) 1   B) 3   C) 7   D) 9

26. The binary tree grows on the Island of Twos. It has 2 branches when it is 1 year old, and it doubles the number of branches each year after this. How many branches will the binary tree have when it is 5 years old?

    A) 5   B) 10   C) 16   D) 32

27. The greatest common divisor of 2×3×5×7 and 2×3×5×11 is

    A) 2×3×5   B) 235
    C) 7×11   D) 2×3×5×7×11

28. A triangular sheet of paper is cut along a straight line into two pieces. Neither of these two pieces can be

    A) an acute triangle   B) a right triangle
    C) a trapezoid   D) a square

29. The length of each side of a rectangle is an even number. The perimeter of this rectangle *cannot* be

    A) 16   B) 136   C) 180   D) 246

30. Each of the six Acrobatic Acropolis Brothers is exactly 180 cm tall. When one stands on any brother's shoulders, together they are 330 cm tall. How tall are they together if they stand on each other's shoulders to make their 6-man human tower?

    A) 900 cm   B) 930 cm   C) 960 cm   D) 990 cm

The end of the contest **5**

Solutions on Page 99 • Answers on Page 144

1993-94 Annual 5th Grade Contest

Spring, 1994
Instructions

5

- **Time** Do *not* open this booklet until you are told by your teacher to begin. You will have only *30 minutes* working time for this contest. You might be *unable* to finish all 30 questions in the time allowed.

- **Scores** Please remember that *this is a contest, not a test*—and there is no "passing" or "failing" score. Few students score as high as 24 points (80% correct). Students with half that, 12 points, *should be commended!*

- **Format and Point Value** This is a multiple-choice contest. Each answer is an A, B, C, or D. Write each answer in the *Answer Column* to the right of each question. A correct answer is worth 1 point. Unanswered questions get no credit. You **may** use a calculator.

1. $22 + 33 + 44 = 3 \times$?

   A) 11   B) 33   C) 99   D) 297

2. Eight eighty-eights equals

   A) 98   B) 704   C) 888   D) 7040

3. $1 \times 2 \times 1 \times 3 \times 1 \times 4 \times 1 \times 5 = 2 \times 3 \times 4 \times 5 \times$?

   A) 1   B) 4   C) 6   D) 8

4. What is the remainder when 10101 is divided by 100?

   A) 0   B) 1   C) 2   D) 3

5. $19 + 29 + 39 + 1 + 1 + 1 = 20 + 30 + 40 +$?

   A) 0   B) 1   C) 3   D) 6

6. The 4940 quarters in my piggybank are worth

   A) \$1235   B) \$2470
   C) \$4940   D) \$19 760

7. $32 - 16 + 16 - 8 + 8 - 4 + 4 - 2 =$

   A) 34   B) 32   C) 30   D) 28

8. Of the following expressions, which one is not equal to $1 \div 1$?

   A) 1×1 B) $2 \div 2$ C) $1 \times 1 \div 1$ D) $1 - 1$

9. What is the average of 7, 8, 9, 10, 11, 12, and 13?

   A) 7   B) 10   C) 17   D) 70

10. In Weird Al's collection of 40 spiders, each spider has 8 legs. What is the total number of legs in Al's spider collection?

    A) 5   B) 48   C) 160   D) 320

11. If today is April 18th, what month will it be in 125 days?

    A) June   B) July   C) August   D) September

12. Equal numbers of 2's and 3's are added together to get 60. What is the total number of 3's used in this sum?

    A) 5   B) 10   C) 12   D) 20

13. $(1 + 1) \times (2 + 2) = 2 +$?

    A) 1   B) 4   C) 6   D) 8

Go on to the next page ⫸ **5**

14. Mary is 10 years old. Mary is 3 years older than Mark, and John is twice as old as Mary. How many years older than Mark is John? A) 7 B) 10 C) 13 D) 20	14.
15. When a certain number is divided by 10, the quotient is 99 and the remainder is 9. What was the original number? A) 11 B) 90 C) 108 D) 999	15.
16. By how much does the number of hours in three full days exceed the number of minutes in one hour? A) 12 B) 36 C) 57 D) 4320	16.
17. How many numbers between 10 and 100 are divisible by 11? A) 8 B) 9 C) 10 D) 11	17.
18. What number do I get if I round 126 to the nearest 10, multiply my result by 2, then round this number to the nearest hundred? A) 200 B) 240 C) 260 D) 300	18.
19. The day that Dad won $9889 in the lottery, Mom won $6776 in the same lottery! Dad won _?_ more than Mom in this lottery. A) $3113 B) $3131 C) $3223 D) $16 665	19.
20. Paula's school usually starts at 8:05 A.M., but tomorrow she must be at school 50 minutes early for a trip to the museum. What is the latest time she should arrive at school tomorrow? A) 6:55 A.M. B) 7:05 A.M. C) 7:15 A.M. D) 7:55 A.M.	20.
21. I own 5 plastic dinosaurs, and each has 4 legs. If I paint 3 stripes on each dinosaur leg, then how many stripes did I paint all together? A) 12 B) 15 C) 20 D) 60	21.
22. Bubble gum comes in packs of 5 pieces of gum. Robin wants to buy bubble gum for herself and her 7 friends, so that each person can have at least two pieces of bubble gum. To do this, what is the least number of packs Robin must buy? A) 2 B) 3 C) 4 D) 5	22.

Go on to the next page ⫸ **5**

23. Which of the following *cannot* be the measure of an angle in a right triangle?

    A) 30° B) 60° C) 90° D) 120°

    23.

24. Gil, Jill, and Bill the Thrill rode the roller coaster. Gil and Jill rode 3 times each. Bill the Thrill rode 9 times. What was the average number of rides they took?

    A) 4   B) 5
    C) 6   D) 12

    24.

25. For any whole number N, let #N be the number of letters it takes to write N as an English word. For example, #18 = 8, since the word "**eighteen**" has 8 letters. For how many whole numbers greater than 0 and less than 1000 does #$N = N$?

    A) 0   B) 1   C) 2   D) 4

    25.

26. Between which of the following pairs of numbers does the greatest number of even numbers occur?

    A) 25 and 141 B) 137 and 245 C) 183 and 297 D) 249 and 363

    26.

27. The triplet plant grows 1 leaf the first month, and then it triples its leaves each month thereafter. If it must have more than 90 leaves before it can be picked, what is the least number of months it must grow before it can be picked?

    A) 5   B) 6   C) 30   D) 31

    27.

28. What is the right-most digit of the product

    $$111 \times 222 \times 333 \times 444 \times 555 \times 666 \times 777 \times 888 \times 999?$$

    A) 0   B) 1   C) 4   D) 6

    28.

29. The number of *zero-digits* in 80500 is 3. If the product $1 \times 2 \times 3 \times 4 \times 5 \times 6 \times 7 \times 8 \times 9 \times 10 = 3628800$, how many *zero-digits* are in the product $10 \times 20 \times 30 \times 40 \times 50 \times 60 \times 70 \times 80 \times 90 \times 100$?

    A) 2   B) 10   C) 12   D) 13

    29.

30. $(200 + 199 + \ldots + 101) - (100 + 99 + \ldots + 1) = 100 \times \underline{?}$

    A) 99   B) 100   C) 199   D) 200

    30.

The end of the contest **5**

1994-95 Annual 5th Grade Contest

Spring, 1995

5

Instructions

- **Time** Do *not* open this booklet until you are told by your teacher to begin. You will have only *30 minutes* working time for this contest. You might be *unable* to finish all 30 questions in the time allowed.

- **Scores** Please remember that *this is a contest, not a test*—and there is no "passing" or "failing" score. Few students score as high as 24 points (80% correct). Students with half that, 12 points, *should be commended!*

- **Format and Point Value** This is a multiple-choice contest. Each answer is an A, B, C, or D. Write each answer in the *Answer Column* to the right of each question. A correct answer is worth 1 point. Unanswered questions get no credit. You **may** use a calculator.

1. If today is Tuesday, 18 days from now will be
   A) Wed. B) Thurs. C) Fri. D) Sat.

   1.

2. $1 \times 11 \times 1 \times 11 \times 1 \times 11 = 11 \times \underline{?}$
   A) 3   B) 11   C) 33   D) 121

   2.

3. If there are 5 vowels in the English alphabet and the
   other letters are all consonants, how many consonants are there?
   A) 21   B) 22   C) 25   D) 26

   3.

4. $600 - (98 + 99 + 100 + 101 + 102) =$
   A) 0   B) 80   C) 100   D) 904

   4.

5. I paid for my lunch with 5 quarters, 5 dimes, and 5 pennies.
   I could have paid for it with $\underline{?}$ nickels.
   A) 8   B) 15   C) 28   D) 36

   5.

6. $4 + 8 + 12 + 16 = (1 + 2 + 3 + 4) \times \underline{?}$
   A) 4   B) 16   C) 18   D) 256

   6.

7. 111 more than 99 is
   A) 12   B) 110   C) 200   D) 210

   7.

8. What is the remainder when $1+41+441+4441$ is divided by 4?
   A) 0   B) 1   C) 2   D) 3

   8.

9. $333 + 333 + 333 + 333 + 333 + 333 = 666 \times \underline{?}$
   A) 1   B) 2   C) 3   D) 6

   9.

10. The product of the first three positive prime numbers is
    A) 6   B) 24   C) 30   D) 105

    10.

11. In a dog race, my dog ran after a
    mail truck and finished 7th best
    (which was also 7th from last).
    If there were no ties, how many
    dogs ran in this race?
    A) 7 B) 13 C) 14 D) 15

    11.

12. Which of the following figures is not a polygon?
    A) a square   B) a circle   C) a triangle   D) a hexagon

    12.

Go on to the next page ⟶ **5**

40

13. Three kids rubbed a magic lamp an average of 13 times each. If one kid rubbed the lamp 13 times, the number of times the other two kids could have rubbed the lamp could *not* have been
A) 10 and 14   B) 11 and 15
C) 0 and 26   D) 9 and 17

13.

14. $1000 \times 100 \times 10 \times 1 \times 0 =$
A) 0   B) 1   C) 1111   D) 1 000 000

14.

15. What is the product of the three odd numbers which are greater than 3 and less than 11?
A) 21   B) 35   C) 105   D) 315

15.

16. Dad held the door closed from 5:59 P.M. to 7:01 P.M. today. How many minutes was that?
A) 52   B) 62   C) 102   D) 122

16.

17. Of the following, which is nearest in value to 10×10?
A) 9×9 B) 9×10 C) 9×11 D) 10×11

17.

18. Ten 10's + nine 9's + eight 8's equals
A) 145   B) 243   C) 245   D) 720

18.

19. For the number 56 789, add the tens' digit to the product of the ten-thousands' and hundreds' digits. What is this sum?
A) 20   B) 43   C) 47   D) 50

19.

20. I shipped some books by Stork Express. I sent half the books on Monday, 8 more on Tuesday, and the final 2 on Wednesday. How many books did I ship altogether?
A) 16   B) 18   C) 20   D) 22

20.

21. The number of seconds in two hours is
A) 120   B) 720   C) 3600   D) 7200

21.

22. $(333\,333\,333\,333\,333) \div 9 =$
A) 37 373 737   B) 37 037 037 037 037
C) 370 370 370 370 370   D) 37 373 737 373 737

22.

Go on to the next page ▐▶ 5

41

23. A square can intersect (cross) a circle in at most _?_ points.

    A) 2   B) 4   C) 6   D) 8

    23.

24. $(100 - 99) \times (99 - 98) \times (98 - 97) \times \ldots \times (3 - 2) \times (2 - 1) =$

    A) 1   B) 5   C) 100   D) 200

    24.

25. An equilateral triangle and a square have a common
    side. If the perimeter of the entire figure is 35,
    then the perimeter of the triangle alone is

    A) 7   B) 15   C) 21   D) 28

    25.

26. A whole number is divided by its largest odd number factor.
    It is *possible* that the resulting quotient equals

    A) 23   B) 36   C) 48   D) 64

    26.

27. A magic carpet ride costs 25¢ per minute
    with a rental phone and 10¢ per minute
    without one. For $2, how many more
    minutes can I fly without renting a
    phone than with renting one?

    A) 8   B) 12
    C) 13   D) 20

    27.

28. The perimeter of the larger of
    two squares is 8 times the perim-
    eter of the smaller. How many of the smaller squares would
    just fit into the larger square, without overlapping each other?

    A) 4   B) 8   C) 16   D) 64

    28.

29. What is the ones' digit of $111 \times 222 \times 333 \times 444 \times 555 \times 666 \times 777$?

    A) 0   B) 1   C) 4   D) 7

    29.

30. If I made a list of every seven-digit whole number greater

    than 1 million which has exactly six of its digits equal to 9,

    how many different numbers would be on my list?

    A) 7   B) 9   C) 62   D) 63

    30.

The end of the contest 👈 **5**

Solutions on Page 107 • Answers on Page 146

1995-96 Annual 5th Grade Contest

Spring, 1996

Instructions

5

- **Time** Do *not* open this booklet until you are told by your teacher to begin. You will have only *30 minutes* working time for this contest. You might be *unable* to finish all 30 questions in the time allowed.

- **Scores** Please remember that *this is a contest, not a test*—and there is no "passing" or "failing" score. Few students score as high as 24 points (80% correct). Students with half that, 12 points, *should be commended!*

- **Format and Point Value** This is a multiple-choice contest. Each answer is an A, B, C, or D. Write each answer in the *Answer Column* to the right of each question. A correct answer is worth 1 point. Unanswered questions get no credit. You **may** use a calculator.

1. $(11 + 11 + 11 + 11 + 11 + 11) - (9 + 9 + 9 + 9 + 9 + 9) =$

   A) 2   B) 6   C) 12   D) 102

   1.

2. Dale needs 44 slices of pizza for a party. If each pizza is cut into 8 slices, then Dale needs at least _?_ pizzas for the party.

   A) 2   B) 4   C) 5   D) 6

   2.

3. $1 \times 5 \times 1 \times 5 \times 1 \times 5 =$

   A) 15   B) 18   C) 45   D) 125

   3.

4. Which figure has one more side than a square?

   A) a circle   B) a pentagon   C) a triangle   D) a rectangle

   4.

5. If a pat on the back costs 25¢, how many such pats can I buy with 5 nickels and 5 dimes?

   A) 2   B) 3   C) 4   D) 5

   5.

6. Of the following, which is the smallest?

   A) $64 \div 64$ B) $64 \div 16$ C) $16 \div 8$ D) $16 \div 1$

   6.

7. Which of the following pairs of numbers does *not* have a greatest common divisor of 2?

   A) 1 & 2   B) 2 & 4   C) 4 & 6   D) 6 & 8

   7.

8. Of the following sums, which is an even number?

   A) $1 + 2 + 4 + 8 + 16$ B) $1 + 2 + 1 + 2 + 1$
   C) $1 + 2 + 3 + 4 + 5$ D) $2 + 4 + 6 + 8 + 10$

   8.

9. Lisa mailed some postcards to 10 of her friends while she was on vacation. She sent three of them 1 postcard each, and the rest of them 2 postcards each. How many postcards did she send in all?

   A) 13   B) 14   C) 17   D) 23

   9.

10. $(77\,777\,777\,777 + 7) \div 7 =$

    A) $11\,111\,111\,112$ B) $11\,111\,111\,111$
    C) $11\,111\,111\,110$ D) $77\,777\,777\,770$

    10.

11. Which is the largest number that is a factor of both 48 and 84?

    A) 4   B) 6   C) 12   D) 24

    11.

Go on to the next page Ⅲ➡ **5**

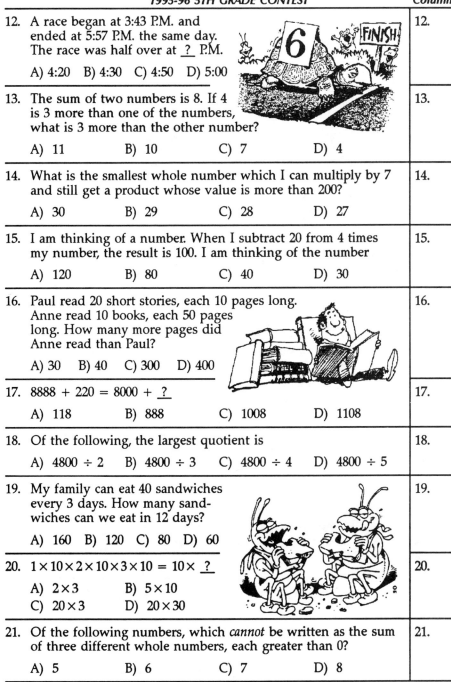

12. A race began at 3:43 P.M. and ended at 5:57 P.M. the same day. The race was half over at _?_ P.M.

    A) 4:20   B) 4:30   C) 4:50   D) 5:00

    12.

13. The sum of two numbers is 8. If 4 is 3 more than one of the numbers, what is 3 more than the other number?

    A) 11   B) 10   C) 7   D) 4

    13.

14. What is the smallest whole number which I can multiply by 7 and still get a product whose value is more than 200?

    A) 30   B) 29   C) 28   D) 27

    14.

15. I am thinking of a number. When I subtract 20 from 4 times my number, the result is 100. I am thinking of the number

    A) 120   B) 80   C) 40   D) 30

    15.

16. Paul read 20 short stories, each 10 pages long. Anne read 10 books, each 50 pages long. How many more pages did Anne read than Paul?

    A) 30   B) 40   C) 300   D) 400

    16.

17. $8888 + 220 = 8000 +$ _?_

    A) 118   B) 888   C) 1008   D) 1108

    17.

18. Of the following, the largest quotient is

    A) $4800 \div 2$ B) $4800 \div 3$ C) $4800 \div 4$ D) $4800 \div 5$

    18.

19. My family can eat 40 sandwiches every 3 days. How many sandwiches can we eat in 12 days?

    A) 160   B) 120   C) 80   D) 60

    19.

20. $1 \times 10 \times 2 \times 10 \times 3 \times 10 = 10 \times$ _?_

    A) 2×3 B) 5×10
    C) 20×3 D) 20×30

    20.

21. Of the following numbers, which *cannot* be written as the sum of three different whole numbers, each greater than 0?

    A) 5   B) 6   C) 7   D) 8

    21.

1995-96 5TH GRADE CONTEST

22. If a camera takes 64 pictures every second, how many pictures does this camera take in 10 minutes?

A) 10×60 B) 64×10 C) 64×60 D) 64×600

22.

23. First, Captain Ahab sailed 200 km across the Moby Sea. Then, he sailed three times as far to Oyster Island. Altogether, he sailed _?_ km.

A) 203   B) 600   C) 800   D) 1200

23.

24. If the perimeter of each square is 8, what is the perimeter of the figure?

A) 8   B) 16   C) 20   D) 24

24.

25. Upon hearing the good news, Lucky counted backwards from 1000 by 7's. One of the numbers Lucky counted was

A) 0   B) 1   C) 3   D) 6

25.

26. If 111 is divided by 4, the product of the quotient and the remainder is

A) 1   B) 30   C) 81   D) 111

26.

27. What is the ones' digit of $5 \times 5 \times 5 \times 5 \times 5 \times 5 \times 5 \times 5 \times 5 \times 5 \times 2$?

A) 0   B) 1   C) 2   D) 5

27.

28. The cost of 1 two-liter bottle of juice is 5 times the cost of 1 can of juice. If 1 two-liter bottle costs 60¢ more than 3 cans, how much does 1 two-liter bottle cost?

A) $1.00   B) $1.20   C) $1.50   D) $1.80

28.

29. If the sum of two consecutive odd numbers is 1000, what is the smaller of the two numbers?

A) 1   B) 499   C) 500   D) 999

29.

30. $(1 + 2 + 3 + \ldots + 49 + 50) + (99 + 98 + 97 + \ldots + 51 + 50) =$

A) 500   B) 5000   C) 5050   D) 5100

30.

The end of the contest ✍ **5**

Solutions on Page 111 • Answers on Page 147

6th Grade Contests

1991-92 through 1995-96

1991-92 Annual 6th Grade Contest

Tuesday, March 10, 1992

Instructions

6

- **Time** You will have only *30 minutes* working time for this contest. You might be *unable* to finish all 40 questions in the time allowed.

- **Scores** Please remember that *this is a contest, not a test*—and there is no "passing" or "failing" score. Few students score as high as 30 points (75% correct). Students with half that, 15 points, *should be commended!*

- **Format and Point Value** This is a multiple-choice contest. Each answer is an A, B, C, or D. Write each answer in the *Answers* column to the right of each question. A correct answer is worth 1 point. Unanswered questions get no credit. You **may** use a calculator.

1. Add the number of days in January, March, April, May, June, July, August, September, October, November, and December. A) 334 B) 335 C) 336 D) 337	1.
2. When (1000 + 900 + 90 + 2) is divided by 5, the remainder is A) 1 B) 2 C) 3 D) 4	2.
3. (100 − 1) + (101 − 2) + (102 − 3) + (103 − 4) = 400 − _?_ . A) 0 B) 3 C) 4 D) 10	3.
4. If an even number is multiplied by 5, the ones' digit of the product is A) 0 B) 1 C) 2 D) 5	4.
5. $10^3 + (10^3 − 10^2) + (10^2 − 10) + (10 − 8) =$ A) 2008 B) 2002 C) 1998 D) 1992	5.
6. Find the missing number: 400 − 100 = _?_ − 50. A) 350 B) 300 C) 200 D) 150	6.
7. The sum of 5 nickels and 5 quarters has the same value as A) 3 dimes B) 8 dimes C) 10 dimes D) 15 dimes	7.
8. 7766 − 6677 = A) 1089 B) 1099 C) 1189 D) 1199	8.
9. Of the following, which has the *most* whole number divisors? A) 16 B) 34 C) 85 D) 121	9.
10. I multiplied my age by 4, added 20, divided by 2, and then subtracted twice my age. What number did I finally get? A) 0 B) 5 C) 10 D) 20	10.
11. In a leap year, the 70th day of the year will be March _?_ . A) 9th B) 10th C) 11th D) 12th	11.
12. Which of these numbers is *not* a factor of $(1 \times 2 \times 3 \times 4 \times 5 \times 6)$? A) 7 B) 8 C) 9 D) 10	12.
13. The average of eight 8's is A) 1 B) 8 C) 64 D) 88	13.
14. Ten-million divided by ten-thousand equals A) 10 B) 100 C) 1000 D) 10000	14.
15. The time 475 minutes after 1:00 P.M. is A) 7:55 P.M. B) 8:45 P.M. C) 8:55 P.M. D) 9:55 P.M.	15.

Go on to the next page ▥▸ **6**

16. $2^8 - 2^7 - 2^6 - 2^5 =$ A) 2^5 B) 2^4 C) 2^3 D) 2^2	16.
17. Mark is twice his sister's age, and she is 6. If their mother's age is twice the sum of their ages, how old is their mother? A) 18 B) 24 C) 32 D) 36	17.
18. The sum of the measures of all the angles of a triangle is A) 180° B) 120° C) 90° D) 60°	18.
19. Which of the following is *not* a factor of 7777? A) 7 B) 77 C) 777 D) 7777	19.
20. If 10% of 10% of a certain number is 2, this certain number is A) 20 B) 100 C) 120 D) 200	20.
21. If the space shuttle circles the earth once every half-hour, then in 24 hours the shuttle will circle the earth _?_ times. A) 48 B) 36 C) 24 D) 12	21.
22. When 57 999 is divided by 58, the quotient is _?_ and the remainder is 57. A) 1 B) 9 C) 99 D) 999	22.
23. The sum of the two prime numbers between 20 and 30 is A) 44 B) 50 C) 52 D) 54	23.
24. $\sqrt{1} + \sqrt{4} + \sqrt{9} + \sqrt{16} =$ A) $\sqrt{10}$ B) $\sqrt{25}$ C) $\sqrt{30}$ D) $\sqrt{100}$	24.
25. The length of a side of a square is _?_% of its perimeter. A) 4 B) 25 C) 40 D) 400	25.
26. A whole number is greater than 20 and less than 2000. What is the *smallest* possible value of the sum of all of its digits? A) 0 B) 1 C) 2 D) 3	26.
27. The greatest common factor of $4 \times 8 \times 12$ and $2 \times 4 \times 6$ is A) 4 B) 8 C) 12 D) 48	27.
28. The *prime* factorization of 72 is A) $2^2 \times 9$ B) $2^3 \times 9$ C) $2^3 \times 3^2$ D) $2^2 \times 3^2$	28.
29. Which of the following symbols can replace the ♦ and convert the statement (77×888) ♦ (88×777) into a true statement? A) < B) = C) > D) ≠	29.
30. Which of the following numbers *cannot* be expressed as the product of two consecutive whole numbers? A) 0 B) 2 C) 56 D) 63	30.

Go on to the next page ⫸ **6**

31. What is the fewest number of squares, each with a perimeter of 4, that would completely cover a square with a side of 4?

    A) 1   B) 4   C) 8   D) 16

31.

32. The sum of five different positive integers is 500. The largest possible value for one of these integers is

    A) 102   B) 490   C) 494   D) 499

32.

33. The average of six numbers is 12. Subtract 6 from one of these numbers. The six numbers would then have an average of

    A) 6   B) 10   C) 11   D) 12

33.

34. I write 1992 different whole numbers. The difference between the *number* of even numbers I wrote and the *number* of odd numbers I wrote can equal any of the following *except*

    A) 0   B) 700   C) 1111   D) 1992

34.

35. The length of each side of a hexagon is a whole number. The perimeter of this hexagon *cannot* equal

    A) 5   B) 1991   C) 1992   D) 1993

35.

36. The difference between two prime numbers can *never* equal

    A) 1   B) 2   C) 7   D) 8

36.

37. A circle and a square intersect so that two sides of the square are also radii of the circle. If a side of the square is 2, what is the area of the shaded region?

    A) $4\pi - 4$ B) $4 - \pi$ C) $2\pi - 4$ D) $\pi - 2$

37.

38. In a list of 200 numbers, each number after the first number is 4 more than the number that comes before it. What is the difference between the first and the last number on this list?

    A) 200   B) 796   C) 800   D) 804

38.

39. The sum of the squares of the first 20 positive integers is 2870. What is the sum of the squares of the first 19 positive integers?

    A) 2350   B) 2361   C) 2470   D) 2850

39.

40. My dog was 100 m from home, and my cat was 80 m from home. I called them, and they both ran directly home. If my dog ran twice as fast as my cat, how far from home was my cat when my dog reached home?

    A) 20 m   B) 30 m   C) 40 m   D) 50 m

40.

The end of the contest ✍ **6**

Solutions on Page 117 • Answers on Page 148

1992-93 Annual 6th Grade Contest

Tuesday, March 9, 1993

Instructions

6

- **Time** You will have only *30 minutes* working time for this contest. You might be *unable* to finish all 40 questions in the time allowed.

- **Scores** Please remember that *this is a contest, not a test*—and there is no "passing" or "failing" score. Few students score as high as 30 points (75% correct). Students with half that, 15 points, *should be commended!*

- **Format and Point Value** This is a multiple-choice contest. Each answer is an A, B, C, or D. Write each answer in the *Answers* column to the right of each question. A correct answer is worth 1 point. Unanswered questions get no credit. You **may** use a calculator.

	Answers
1. $900 + 90 + 9 + 1 =$ A) 100 B) 991 C) 1000 D) 9000	1.
2. If six days ago was a Tuesday, then eight days from today is a A) Monday B) Tuesday C) Wednesday D) Thursday	2.
3. Find the missing number: $12345 + 123450 = 12345 \times \underline{\,?\,}$ A) 2 B) 10 C) 11 D) 22	3.
4. There are 30 students in Pat's math class. If there are twice as many girls as boys in the class, how many boys are in the class? A) 5 B) 8 C) 10 D) 20	4.
5. Find the missing number: $512 \times 2 = 32 \times \underline{\,?\,}$ A) 4 B) 8 C) 16 D) 32	5.
6. If the area of the rectangle shown at the right is 24, what is its perimeter? **4** A) 10 B) 16 C) 20 D) 24	6.
7. $(2 + 4 + 6 + 8 + 10) \div (10 + 8 + 6 + 4 + 2) =$ A) 0 B) 1 C) 2 D) 60	7.
8. Twice my house number, plus 4, is 18. What's my house number? A) 5 B) 7 C) 14 D) 40	8.
9. $11 + 12 + 13 + 14 + 15 = 1 + 2 + 3 + 4 + 5 + \underline{\,?\,}$ A) 10 B) 50 C) 60 D) 65	9.
10. (Number of sides of a pentagon) + (number of sides of a trapezoid) − (number of sides of a hexagon) = number of sides of $\underline{\,?\,}$ A) a triangle B) a square C) a pentagon D) an octagon	10.
11. $99 \times 9 =$ A) $990 - 9$ B) $990 - 90$ C) $900 - 99$ D) $900 - 9$	11.
12. The ratio of a side of a square to its perimeter is always A) 2:1 B) 1:1 C) 1:2 D) 1:4	12.
13. The product of *all* the prime numbers less than 10 is divisible by A) 70 B) 60 C) 12 D) 4	13.
14. Find the missing number: $64 \div 2 = 2 \times \underline{\,?\,}$ A) 16 B) 32 C) 64 D) 128	14.
15. $3^2 + 3^2 + 3^2 + 3^2 =$ A) 4^2 B) 6^2 C) 12^2 D) 33^2	15.

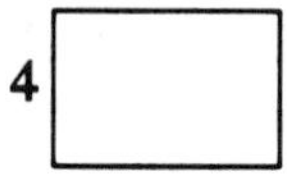

Go on to the next page ⟫ **6**

16. What is the sum of the ten-thousands' digit and the millions' digit of 1 234 567 890? A) 7 B) 9 C) 10 D) 11	16.
17. How many edges does a cube have? A) 6 B) 8 C) 10 D) 12	17.
18. A balloon ride can take at most 3 people at a time. If 41 people want to fly in the balloon, the least number of rides needed is A) 12 B) 13 C) 14 D) 15	18.
19. What is the average of 1, 2, 3, 4, 5, 6, 7, 8, and 9? A) 5 B) 6 C) 9 D) 45	19.
20. Ali, Barb, and Cal were all born on April 1, in different years. This coming April 1, if I add all their ages together, I'll get 9. On that day, Ali's age could *not* be ? A) 7 B) 5 C) 3 D) 1	20.
21. The lengths of the three sides of a triangle *could* be . A) 0, 1, 2 B) 1, 2, 3 C) 2, 3, 4 D) 2, 4, 6	21.
22. If a whole number is multiplied by itself, the ones' digit of the product *cannot* be A) 1 B) 5 C) 7 D) 9	22.
23. What is the greatest common divisor of $3 \times 6 \times 9$ and $30 \times 60 \times 90$? A) 3 B) $3 \times 6 \times 9$ C) $30 \times 60 \times 90$ D) $10 \times 3 \times 6 \times 9$	23.
24. A string 12 meters long is cut into 6 pieces of equal length. What is the sum of the lengths of any 4 of these pieces? A) 2 m B) 4 m C) 6 m D) 8 m	24.
25. What is the smallest prime number greater than 47? A) 59 B) 57 C) 53 D) 51	25.
26. $\sqrt{9+16+144} = \sqrt{9} + \sqrt{16} +$? A) $\sqrt{36}$ B) $\sqrt{100}$ C) $\sqrt{144}$ D) $\sqrt{169}$	26.
27. Martha had $1.50. She bought 12 caramels at 5¢ each. How many chocolate mints at 10¢ each can she buy with the money she has left? A) 12 B) 11 C) 10 D) 9	27.
28. If 1000% of a certain number is 100, the certain number is A) 1 B) 10 C) 100 D) 1000	28.
29. Two whole numbers differ by 1. If one number has 3 digits and the other has 4 digits, what is their sum? A) 1001 B) 1100 C) 1999 D) 2001	29.

Go on to the next page ⮕ **6**

30. Jodie has just begun to read a 160-page book. If she reads 20 pages every day, she will finish the book in A) 8 days B) 18 days C) 20 days D) 80 days	30.
31. Ten years ago, the sum of the ages of my mother and father was 71. What is the sum of their ages today? A) 51 B) 61 C) 81 D) 91	31.
32. A family made a 100 km trip. For half the distance, they drove at 50 km per hour; for the other half, they drove at 25 km per hour. How many hours did this trip take? A) 3 B) 4 C) 5 D) 6	32.
33. If this is March, what month will it be 1993 months from today? A) January B) February C) March D) April	33.
34. If 2 dogs weigh as much as 3 cats, and 2 cats weigh as much as 15 mice, how many dogs weigh as much as 45 mice? A) 3 B) 4 C) 6 D) 9	34.
35. The sum of the digits of 1993 is 1+9+9+3, or 22. At some time in the future, the sum of the digits of a year will be 33. This will *first* occur in the _?_ century. A) 21st B) 60th C) 70th D) 80th	35.
36. The shaded area of rectangle *ABCD* is twice as large as the unshaded area. If the unshaded area is 12, what is the area of *ABCD*? A) 36 B) 30 C) 24 D) 18	36.
37. The time on a 12-hour circular clock is 11:00 A.M. When the *minute* hand goes around 3 times, the time will be A) 11:03 A.M. B) 11:30 A.M. C) 1:00 P.M. D) 2:00 P.M.	37.
38. The sum of the first 100 positive even whole numbers is 10 100. What is the sum of the first 101 positive even whole numbers? A) 10 302 B) 10 202 C) 10 201 D) 10 102	38.
39. My pay is the same every day I work. I worked *every* day in 1992, even weekends. In March, I earned $930. I earned _?_ for all of 1992. A) $11 346 B) $11 315 C) $10 980 D) $10 950	39.
40. Which of the following numbers *cannot* be written as the sum of 4 consecutive whole numbers? A) 1994 B) 2042 C) 2050 D) 2060	40.

The end of the contest **6**

Solutions on Page 121 • Answers on Page 149

1993-94 Annual 6th Grade Contest

Tuesday, March 8, 1994

Instructions

6

- **Time** You will have only *30 minutes* working time for this contest. You might be *unable* to finish all 40 questions in the time allowed.

- **Scores** Please remember that *this is a contest, not a test*—and there is no "passing" or "failing" score. Few students score as high as 30 points (75% correct). Students with half that, 15 points, *should be commended!*

- **Format and Point Value** This is a multiple-choice contest. Each answer is an A, B, C, or D. Write each answer in the *Answers* column to the right of each question. A correct answer is worth 1 point. Unanswered questions get no credit. You **may** use a calculator.

1. $51 + 49 + 51 + 49 + 51 + 49 + 51 + 49 =$ A) 104 B) 400 C) 440 D) 800	1.
2. If a mischievous bookworm eats one book every 5 minutes for one hour, how many books does it eat during this hour? A) 60 B) 30 C) 24 D) 12	2.
3. $1 \times 1 + 1 \times 0 =$ A) 0 B) 1 C) 2 D) 3	3.
4. The "Thought–I–Could" train comes to town every day at 6 A.M. Between 11 A.M. Tuesday and 11 P.M. Friday, how many times does this train come to town? A) 3 B) 4 C) 5 D) 6	4.
5. $456 + 456 + 456 + 456 + 456 + 456 + 456 + 456 + 456 + 456 =$ A) 466 B) 4104 C) 4560 D) 5016	5.
6. Of the following numbers, which is *not* a factor of $999 - 9$? A) 9 B) 10 C) 11 D) 12	6.
7. What is the remainder when $5 + 10 + 15 + 20 + 1 + 1 + 1 + 1 + 1$ is divided by 5? A) 0 B) 1 C) 2 D) 4	7.
8. $6 + 5 \times [4 + 3 \times (2 + 1)] =$ A) 61 B) 71 C) 143 D) 231	8.
9. What is 0.9949, rounded to the nearest hundredth? A) 0.99 B) 0.994 C) 0.995 D) 1.00	9.
10. $(1 \times 10^3) + (99 \times 10) + (4 \times 1) =$ A) 1904 B) 1994 C) 1995 D) 2904	10.
11. In the word *lunchtime*, what is the ratio of the number of vowels to the total number of letters? A) 3:10 B) 2:3 C) 1:2 D) 1:3	11.
12. When _?_ is subtracted from 2000, the result is 1245. A) 865 B) 855 C) 765 D) 755	12.
13. $(41 \times 42) - (42 \times 40) =$ A) 40 B) 41 C) 42 D) 84	13.
14. On a trip, Pat fished every day. Pat's trip began on the morning of August 12, and ended on the night of August 25. Pat fished for _?_ days on that trip. A) 12 B) 13 C) 14 D) 15	14.
15. $(20 + 30) \div (2 + 3) =$ A) 5 B) 10 C) 20 D) 55	15.

Go on to the next page ⫸ **6**

			Answers
16. One million divided by one hundred = A) 100 B) 1000 C) 10 000 D) 100 000			16.
17. $(8 \times 1000) + (7 \times 100) + (6 \times 10) + (5 \times 1) =$ A) 26 000 B) 8765 C) 1136 D) 26			17.
18. Sue is 11 years old and her sister is 7 years old. What will be the sum of their ages when Sue is 26 years old? A) 33 B) 44 C) 45 D) 48			18.
19. $11 000 + 1100 + 110 + 11 = 11 \times \underline{\ ?\ }$ A) 1101 B) 1111 C) 1121 D) 1 010 101			19.
20. What time will it be 345 minutes after 3:45 P.M.? A) 7:30 P.M. B) 8:30 P.M. C) 9:30 P.M. D) 10:30 P.M.			20.
21. Seventy-seven 77's equals A) 7×7×11×11 B) 7×7×7×7 C) 7×11 D) 7777			21.
22. Two squares share a common side, as shown. If the distance from A to B is 4, what is the perimeter of rectangle ABCD? A) 10 B) 12 C) 14 D) 16			22.
23. Don borrowed 9 quarters from Joe. The next day, Don gave Joe 25 nickels. How much does Don still owe Joe? A) 10 dimes B) 2 quarters C) 2 dollars D) 25¢			23.
24. Which of the following is divisible by 15? A) 35×8 B) 36×9 C) 39×10 D) 40×11			24.
25. If I round 1315 to the nearest ten, then multiply the result by 3, then round to the nearest hundred, what is my final result? A) 3900 B) 3945 C) 3960 D) 4000			25.
26. Each of the following ratios is equal to 3:4 *except* A) 13:14 B) 15:20 C) 33:44 D) 120:160			26.
27. $(10 000 - 1000) + (1000 - 100) + (100 - 10) + (10 - 1) =$ A) 999 B) 9000 C) 9999 D) 99 999			27.
28. The average of four 8's and four 16's equals the average of four $\underline{\ ?\ }$. A) 12's B) 24's C) 48's D) 96's			28.
29. $\frac{1}{3} + \frac{1}{2} + \frac{1}{3} + \frac{1}{2} + \frac{1}{3} =$ A) $\frac{1}{13}$ B) $\frac{5}{13}$ C) $\frac{5}{6}$ D) 2			29.
30. In a right triangle, the sum of the degree measures of the two smaller angles is what percent of the measure of the right angle? A) 45% B) 50% C) 90% D) 100%			30.

Go on to the next page ⫸ **6**

59

31. What is the ones' digit in the product of $19 \times 94 \times 123456789$? A) 2 B) 4 C) 6 D) 8	31.
32. If an equal number of 3's, 5's, and 7's are added together to get 105, what is the total number of 3's used in the sum? A) 7 B) 10 C) 21 D) 71	32.
33. On a 50-question test, Dave got 80% of the questions right, and Janet got 90% of them right. How many more correct answers did Janet get than Dave? A) 1 B) 5 C) 10 D) 45	33.
34. Mike needs 1302 bricks to build a big new brick barbecue to replace his small metal one. If 3 bricks weigh 2 kg, how many kg of bricks does he need? A) 217 B) 434 C) 651 D) 868	34.
35. How many whole numbers greater than 1000 and less than 5000 *cannot* be written as the sum of two odd numbers? A) 0 B) 1 C) 1999 D) 2000	35.
36. Pat and Lee counted leaves on two plants. Pat's count was a 1-digit number. Lee got a 3-digit number. If the difference between their numbers was 91, what was the sum of their numbers? A) 100 B) 109 C) 191 D) 200	36.
37. How many whole numbers between 1 and 500 are divisible by 6 but are not divisible by 8? A) 83 B) 73 C) 63 D) 53	37.
38. Square *ABCD* has a perimeter of 8. If a circle is inscribed in the square, as shown, what is the area of the circle? A) π B) 2π C) 4π D) 16π	38.
39. If $1 \times 2 \times 3 \times 4 \times 5 \times 6 \times 7 \times 8 \times 9 \times 10 \times 11 \times 12 \times 13 \times 14 \times 15 = 1\,307\,674\,368\,000$, how many times does the digit "0" appear in the product $10 \times 20 \times 30 \times 40 \times 50 \times 60 \times 70 \times 80 \times 90 \times 100 \times 110 \times 120 \times 130 \times 140 \times 150$? A) 15 B) 18 C) 19 D) 20	39.
40. For any number *N*, let #(*N*) be the number of prime numbers less than or equal to *N*. What is #(8620) − #(8614)? A) 0 B) 1 C) 2 D) 3	40.

The end of the contest 🖎 **6**

Solutions on Page 125 • Answers on Page 150

1994-95 Annual 6th Grade Contest

Tuesday, March 14, 1995

Instructions

6

- **Time** You will have only *30 minutes* working time for this contest. You might be *unable* to finish all 40 questions in the time allowed.

- **Scores** Please remember that *this is a contest, not a test*—and there is no "passing" or "failing" score. Few students score as high as 30 points (75% correct). Students with half that, 15 points, *should be commended!*

- **Format and Point Value** This is a multiple-choice contest. Each answer is an A, B, C, or D. Write each answer in the *Answers* column to the right of each question. A correct answer is worth 1 point. Unanswered questions get no credit. You **may** use a calculator.

1.	$1000 + 0 + 900 + 0 + 90 + 0 + 5 + 0 =$ A) 1995 B) 19 950 C) 199 500 D) 1 995 000	1.
2.	Which number is nine hundred less than one thousand one? A) 99 B) 100 C) 101 D) 1901	2.
3.	A triangle has sides of lengths 2, 2, and 3. This triangle is A) scalene B) isosceles C) right D) equilateral	3.
4.	This year, there were $11 \times 121 - 11 \times 11$ fewer turkeys eaten than last year. How many fewer turkeys were eaten this year? A) 120 B) 121 C) 1200 D) 1210	4.
5.	200% of 50% equals A) 1% B) 100% C) 250% D) 10 000%	5.
6.	$(1995 + 1994 + 1993) - (1992 + 1991 + 1990) = 1990 - \underline{\ ?\ }$ A) 1999 B) 1993 C) 1987 D) 1981	6.
7.	How many positive primes have remainder 0 when divided by 2? A) 0 B) 1 C) 2 D) 7	7.
8.	Divide $(1+4)+(1+8)+(1+12)+(1+16)$ by 4. The remainder is A) 0 B) 1 C) 2 D) 3	8.
9.	All the figures below consist of the same four squares of equal size. Which figure has the smallest perimeter? A) B) C) D)	9.
10.	The greatest common divisor of 999 999 and $2 \times 2 \times 2 \times 2 \times 2 \times 2$ is A) 1 B) 2 C) 3 D) 9	10.
11.	What number, when added to 1111, results in a sum of 10100? A) 8989 B) 9090 C) 9191 D) 11211	11.
12.	A flapjack flipping chef trainee "missed" $4 - 0 \times 2 - 0 \times 1$ times. How many "misses" is that? A) 0 B) 2 C) 4 D) 8	12.
13.	Of the following, which is *not* a polygon? A) triangle B) rhombus C) pentagon D) circle	13.
14.	$111111 + 111111 + 111111 + 111111 + 111111 + \underline{222222} =$ A) 1 111 111 B) 333 333 C) 666 666 D) 777 777	14.
15.	Pat wrote a word in secret code. In this code, the number 26 stood for the letter "A," the number 25 stood for "B," and so on. In this code, the 5 numbers 19 26 11 11 2 stand for the word A) RATTY B) HAPPY C) HOPPY D) DANNY	15.

Go on to the next page ⯈ **6**

16. 10 quarters + 10 nickels + 10 pennies has the same value as A) 11 dimes B) 21 dimes C) 30 dimes D) 31 dimes	16.
17. To the nearest hundred years, how old is a 3456-year-old Woolly Mammoth? A) 3000 B) 3400 C) 3500 D) 3460	17.
18. $(10 \div 1) + (20 \div 2) + (30 \div 3) + (40 \div 4) = \underline{\ ?\ } \div 5.$ A) 200 B) 100 C) 40 D) 8	18.
19. If the product of an even number and an odd number is 840, what is the largest possible value of this odd number? A) 21 B) 35 C) 105 D) 420	19.
20. What is the sum of the two largest primes less than 30? A) 48 B) 52 C) 56 D) 68	20.
21. $8 \div 4 \times 2 + 4 \times 2 \div 8 =$ A) 2 B) 3 C) 4 D) 5	21.
22. A bakery lowered its price for cookies from 25¢ each to 20¢ each. For $4, how many more cookies could you buy now than before? A) 1 B) 4 C) 5 D) 20	22.
23. Thirty-three minutes after 11 A.M. is $\underline{\ ?\ }$ minutes before 1 P.M. A) 27 B) 87 C) 93 D) 97	23.
24. The average of 7 whole numbers is 7. If 6 of these numbers are 1, then the seventh number must be A) 1 B) 7 C) 13 D) 43	24.
25. $5 \times 5 \times 5 \times 2 \times 2 \times 2 \times 2 \times 2 = 4 \times \underline{\ ?\ }$ A) 125 B) 125×2 C) 125×4 D) 125×8	25.
26. Bob has only enough paint to cover a wall 12m by 15m. At most how many different squares of size 3m by 3m can he paint on that wall? A) 9 B) 18 C) 20 D) 60	26.
27. 1995199519951995 ÷ 1995 = A) 1111 B) 1010101 C) 1001001001 D) 1000100010001	27.
28. If 5 widgets = 10 fidgets, then 8 fidgets = $\underline{\ ?\ }$ widgets. A) 3 B) 4 C) 13 D) 16	28.
29. An isosceles right triangle must have an angle of measure A) 10° B) 40° C) 45° D) 100°	29.

Go on to the next page ⟹ **6**

63

30. Of the following, which has an odd quotient when divided by 2?   30.

    A) 456 456 456 456 456   B) 678 678 678 678 678
    C) 432 432 432 432 432   D) 876 876 876 876 876

31. As shown, *ABCD* is a square and *ADE* is an equilateral triangle. What is the degree-measure of angle *BAE*?   31.

    A) 30° B) 45° C) 60° D) 90°

32. Each of the following ratios is equal to 15 : 60 *except*   32.

    A) $\frac{1}{2}$: 2   B) 11111 : 44444 C) 1 : $\frac{1}{4}$ D) $10^6 : (4 \times 10^6)$

33. Lee multiplied three different prime numbers together. How many different whole numbers are factors of this product?   33.

    A) 3   B) 6   C) 8   D) 9

34. $(1995-1993) \times (1993-1991) \times (1991-1989) \times \ldots \times (5-3) \times (3-1) =$ 34.

    A) 2×996 B) 2×997 C) 2^{996} D) 2^{997}

35. The lengths of a side of square *S* and a radius of circle *C* are equal. What is the area of *C* divided by the area of *S*?   35.

    A) π B) 2π C) 4π D) 4

36. The product of 6 whole numbers is 36. What is the least possible value of their sum?   36.

    A) 8   B) 12   C) 14   D) 16

37. If the pattern of the first 6 letters in *CIRCUSCIRCUS* . . . continues, then the pattern's 500th letter is   37.

    A) *R*   B) *U*   C) *C*   D) *I*

38. I made a list of three-digit whole numbers, and every digit I used was odd. At most how many different numbers were on my list?   38.

    A) 125   B) 150   C) 333   D) 450

39. $2^{1000} + 2^{1000} =$ 39.

    A) 2^{1001} B) 2^{2000} C) 4^{1000} D) 4^{2000}

40. I multiplied one whole number by 18. I multiplied a second whole number by 21. I then added the two products. Of the following, which *could* have been the resulting sum?   40.

    A) 1996 B) 1997 C) 1998 D) 1999

The end of the contest ✍ **6**

Solutions on Page 129 • Answers on Page 151

1995-96 Annual 6th Grade Contest

Tuesday, March 12, 1996

Instructions

6

- **Time** You will have only *30 minutes* working time for this contest. You might be *unable* to finish all 40 questions in the time allowed.

- **Scores** Please remember that *this is a contest, not a test*—and there is no "passing" or "failing" score. Few students score as high as 30 points (75% correct). Students with half that, 15 points, *should be commended!*

- **Format and Point Value** This is a multiple-choice contest. Each answer is an A, B, C, or D. Write each answer in the *Answers* column to the right of each question. A correct answer is worth 1 point. Unanswered questions get no credit. You **may** use a calculator.

1. My friend and I have an average of 64¢ each. We have a total of
   A) 16¢   B) 32¢   C) 64¢   D) $1.28

   1.

2. If I rode two dozen sheep,
   how many sheep did I ride?
   A) 20   B) 24   C) 40   D) 48

   2.

3. Factored into primes, 56 =
   A) 2×28 B) $2 \times 2 \times 14$
   C) $2 \times 4 \times 7$ D) $2 \times 2 \times 2 \times 7$

   3.

4. $777\,777\,777\,770 \div 77\,777\,777\,777 =$
   A) 10   B) 7   C) 1   D) 0

   4.

5. If today is Tuesday, then 31 days ago it was
   A) Friday   B) Saturday   C) Sunday   D) Monday

   5.

6. Each equilateral triangle shown has a perimeter
   of 6. What is the perimeter of the figure?
   A) 6   B) 8   C) 10   D) 12

   6.

7. Of the following, which has the smallest remainder?
   A) $7772 \div 7$ B) $6663 \div 6$ C) $5554 \div 5$ D) $4445 \div 4$

   7.

8. $444 + 333 + 222 + 111 - 999 = 111 \times \underline{\ ?\ }$
   A) 1   B) 2   C) 3   D) 4

   8.

9. A $\underline{\ ?\ }$ does not have two pairs of parallel sides.
   A) square   B) rectangle   C) trapezoid   D) rhombus

   9.

10. $1 \times 1 + 1 \times 9 + 1 \times 9 + 1 \times 6 =$
    A) 25   B) 29   C) 1032   D) 1996

    10.

11. Jan wanted to add 57 and 199, but added 60 and 200 instead.
    What must Jan now subtract to get the sum of 57 and 199?
    A) 1   B) 2   C) 3   D) 4

    11.

12. $22 \times 10 + 22 \times 10^2 + 22 \times 10^3$ has the same value as
    A) 22×10^5 B) 22×10^6 C) 22×1110 D) 22×1111

    12.

13. If one can of paint covers 5 m^2, then
    I'd need at least $\underline{\ ?\ }$ cans to paint four
    walls, each 3 m high and 6 m long.
    A) 4   B) 7
    C) 14   D) 15

    13.

14. $1 \times 9 \times 81 = 3 \times 27 \times \underline{\ ?\ }$
    A) 1   B) 3   C) 9   D) 27

    14.

15. A $\underline{\ ?\ }$ has twice as many sides as a triangle.
    A) hexagon   B) pentagon   C) trapezoid   D) rhombus

    15.

Go on to the next page ▐▐▶ **6**

16. The Binary Berry Bush has twice as many berries each year as the previous year. If it has 1 berry when it is one year old, then at least how old must it be to have more than 100 berries?
    A) 7 years   B) 8 years   C) 49 years   D) 50 years

    16.

17. If my clock stopped running 333 minutes after 2:27 P.M., it stopped running at
    A) 5:00 P.M.   B) 6:00 P.M.
    C) 7:00 P.M.   D) 8:00 P.M.

    17.

18. When $(1000 + 200 + 30 + 4) \times 9$ is simplified, the ones' digit is
    A) 6   B) 7   C) 8   D) 9

    18.

19. When I rounded 13 955 to the nearest ten, hundred, thousand, and ten thousand, _?_ was *not* one of my rounded numbers.
    A) 10 000   B) 13 960   C) 13 900   D) 14 000

    19.

20. Divide $(1+4) \times (1+8) \times (1+12) \times (1+16)$ by 4. The remainder is
    A) 0   B) 1   C) 2   D) 3

    20.

21. Of the following, which ratio is equivalent to $33:11$?
    A) $(3 \div 3):(1 \div 1)$ B) $(1 + 33):(1 + 11)$
    C) $(3 \times 3):(1 \times 1)$ D) $(3 + 3):(1 + 1)$

    21.

22. Which of the following numbers is *not* a factor of $3 \times 5 \times 7$?
    A) 15   B) 21   C) 30   D) 35

    22.

23. My 12 coins, all nickels and dimes, are worth $1.00 all together. How many of my coins are nickels?
    A) 2   B) 4   C) 6   D) 8

    23.

24. $12345654321^2 \div 12345654321 =$
    A) 12345654321   B) 12345654321^2 C) 1   D) 2

    24.

25. If the frame of a ferris wheel is a circle with a 10 m diameter, what is the circumference of this circle?
    A) 5π m   B) 10π m   C) 20π m   D) 25π m

    25.

26. Of 30 students, 12 play football, 17 play soccer, and 5 play both. How many play neither?
    A) 1   B) 4   C) 6   D) 11

    26.

27. $50 \times 40 \times 30 \times 20 \times 10 = 5 \times 4 \times 3 \times 2 \times 1 \times \underline{\ ?\ }$
    A) 10   B) 50   C) 10 000   D) 100 000

    27.

28. Of the following, _?_ have the *largest* least common multiple.
    A) 5 and 7   B) 3 and 15   C) 6 and 8   D) 6 and 9

    28.

29. Which number's positive factors add up to twice the number?
    A) 8   B) 12   C) 24   D) 28

    29.

Go on to the next page ⫸ **6**

67

30. If the lengths of the sides of the squares at the right are 2 and 4, what is the perimeter of the figure? 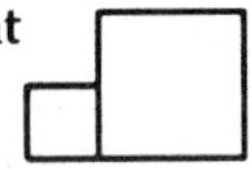
    A) 18   B) 20   C) 22   D) 24 | 30.

31. Pat has $30 to play miniature golf. Games are $4 each, or $8 for three games. What is the greatest number of games Pat can play with $30?
    A) 7   B) 9   C) 10   D) 12 | 31.

32. $\sqrt{4 \times 4} \times \sqrt{4 \times 4} =$
    A) 4   B) 8   C) 16   D) 64 | 32.

33. Maria is 160 cm tall. If she drinks a magic potion that makes her 20% of her height, how tall will she be?
    A) 8 cm   B) 32 cm   C) 128 cm   D) 3200 cm | 33.

34. In a camel herd with 80 legs, half the camels have one hump and half have two. How many humps are there in this herd?
    A) 20   B) 30   C) 60   D) 120 | 34.

35. There are 30 students in a gym class. Of the following, which *could* be the ratio of boys to girls?
    A) 2:3   B) 3:5   C) 2:6   D) 3:4 | 35.

36. If $1 + 2 + 3 + \ldots + 99 + 100 = 5050$, what is the value of $1000-1 + 1000-2 + 1000-3 + \ldots + 1000-99 + 1000-100$?
    A) 4050   B) 40 050   C) 94 950   D) 95 950 | 36.

37. How many different rectangles are in the figure at the right? [NOTE: A square *is* a rectangle.] 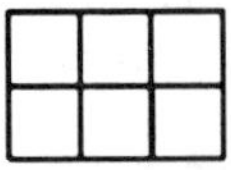
    A) 15   B) 16   C) 17   D) 18 | 37.

38. A 13×13 grid is "checkerboarded" with 13 rows and 13 columns of alternating black and white squares, as partially shown. If the corner square is black, what fraction of the squares are black? 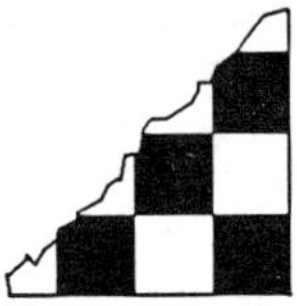
    A) $\frac{85}{169}$ B) $\frac{84}{169}$ C) $\frac{1}{2}$ D) $\frac{2}{3}$ | 38.

39. If each small circle has a diameter of 6, and if each passes through the center of the large circle, what is the area of the shaded region? 
    A) 18π B) 27π C) 72π D) 108π | 39.

40. Lee counted by 7's beginning with one of the whole numbers from 1 through 7, until Lee passed 1000. If Lee counted three of the following numbers, which number did Lee *not* count?
    A) 107   B) 184   C) 534   D) 641 | 40.

The end of the contest ✍ **6**

Solutions on Page 133 • Answers on Page 152

68

Detailed Solutions

• • • • • • • • • • • • • • • • •

1991-92 through 1995-96

4th Grade Solutions

1991-92 through 1995-96

Information & Solutions

Spring, 1992

Contest Information

4

- **Solutions** Turn the page for detailed contest solutions (written in the question boxes) and letter answers (written in the *Answer Column* to the right of each question).

- **Scores** Please remember that *this is a contest, not a test*—and there is no "passing" or "failing" score. Few students score as high as 24 points (80% correct). Students with half that, 12 points, *deserve commendation!*

- **Answers & Rating Scale** Turn to page 138 for the letter answers to each question and the rating scale for this contest.

1991-92 4TH GRADE CONTEST SOLUTIONS

Solution	Answer Column
1. The sum of *any* number of zeroes is 0. A) 0 B) 1 C) 10 D) 11	1. A
2. If, five years ago, I was 5 years old, then today I am 10 years old. Five years from now, I will be 15 years old. A) 10 B) 15 C) 20 D) 25	2. B
3. $1+2+3+4 = 11-10 + 12-10 + 13-10 + 14-10 = 11+12+13+14-40$. A) 10 B) 15 C) 40 D) 50	3. C
4. Ten-thousand divided by two-thousand $= 10 \div 2 = 5$. A) 5 B) 20 C) 5000 D) 8000	4. A
5. $2 + 2 + 2 + 2 = 8 = 2\times2\times2$. A) 2 B) 2×2 C) $2\times2\times2$ D) $2\times2\times2\times2$	5. C
6. 7777 is *exactly* divisible by 7, so 7778 leaves a remainder of 1. A) 0 B) 1 C) 2 D) 8	6. B
7. Since $30 \times 40 = 1200$ and $3\times4 = 12$, $30\times40 = 3\times4\times100$. A) 0 B) 10 C) 100 D) 400	7. C
8. Add an odd and an even number to get an odd number. A) 51 + 51 B) 36 + 63 C) 12 + 24 D) 49 + 51	8. B
9. If I have three dozen pens, then I have $3\times12 = 36$ pens. A) 30 B) 36 C) 39 D) 42	9. B
10. $1 \times 9 \times 9 \times 2 = 9\times9\times2 = 81\times2 = 162$. A) 21 B) 162 C) 180 D) 1992	10. B
11. The whole numbers less than 1000 are 0, 1, 2, 3, . . . , 999. A) 997 B) 998 C) 999 D) 1000	11. D
12. If today is Monday, every 7 days is another Monday. A) Monday B) Tuesday C) Friday D) Sunday	12. A

Go on to the next page ➡ **4**

13. In the list of numbers 1, 2, 3, 4, 5, 6, 7, 8, 9, all the numbers in the list *except* 1 and 2 are exactly 2 more than some other number in the list. For example 6 is 2 more than 4.

    A) 2   B) 7   C) 9   D) 11

13. B

14. If bubble gum costs 5¢ per piece, the number of pieces that Ali can buy for \$2.00 is $200 \div 5 = 40$.

    A) 10   B) 20   C) 40   D) 195

14. C

15. The number must be $51 \div 3 = 17$.

    A) 153   B) 27   C) 17   D) 16

15. C

16. $(1993 - 1992) \div (1992 - 1991) = 1 \div 1 = 1$.

    A) 0   B) 1   C) 1991   D) 1992

16. B

17. Since Jill is 2 cm taller than John, and John is 3 cm taller than Jim, Jill is 5 cm taller than Jim.

    A) 5 cm taller   B) 5 cm shorter
    C) 1 cm taller   D) 1 cm shorter

17. A

18. Since half of a year is 6 months, and 6 years is $6 \times 12 = 72$ months, six and one-half years $= 6 + 72 = 78$ months.

    A) 65   B) 68   C) 72   D) 78

18. D

19. On a sheet of paper, a line is drawn through the center C of a square. As shown, this line intersects (or crosses) the square twice.

    A) 0   B) 1   C) 2   D) 3

19. C

20. The product gets larger as the numbers get closer.

    A) 47×53 B) 48×52 C) 49×51 D) 50×50

20. D

21. 16 minutes *before* 3:15 P.M. is 1 minute before 3:00 P.M.

    A) 2:59 P.M.   B) 2:99 P.M.   C) 3:59 P.M.   D) 4:59 P.M.

21. A

22. $1234 + 5678 = 1200 + 30 + 4 + 5600 + 70 + 8 = 6800 + (30 + 70) + 8 + 4 = 6912$.

    A) 6666   B) 6789   C) 6912   D) 7032

22. C

Go on to the next page ⇒ **4**

23. If I am going to retire when I am 65 years old, and that is 30 years from now, my present age is 65–30 = 35.

    A) 20   B) 25   C) 30   D) 35

    23. D

24. If special stamps cost 17¢ each, then 8 of these stamps cost 8×17¢ = 136¢ = $1.36.

    A) 25¢   B) 56¢   C) $1.26   D) $1.36

    24. D

25. (50–40)+(40–30)+(30–20)+(20–10)=10+10+10+10=40=50–10.

    A) 50   B) 50 – 10   C) 50 + 10   D) 50 × 10

    25. B

26. The *largest* 4-digit even number using these digits exactly once each ends in an 8 and is 9758. The tens' digit is 5.

    A) 9   B) 8   C) 7   D) 5

    26. D

27. When it's divided by 3, the quotient is 240. When divided by twice as much, 6, the quotient is half as large—it's 120.

    A) 720   B) 480   C) 120   D) 80

    27. C

28. The boy becomes 4 cm shorter each year. At age 10, he is 2 m = 200 cm tall. At age 25 years, he will have become 15×4 = 60 cm shorter. His height is then 200 cm – 60 cm = 140 cm.

    A) 140 cm   B) 100 cm   C) 60 cm   D) 40 cm

    28. A

29. If the 1000 whole numbers consist of 999 1's and the number 1000, their product will be 1000 and their sum will be 1999.

    A) 1000   B) 1992   C) 1993   D) 1999

    29. D

30. The perimeter of a small square is 4, so one "small side" is 1. Square *ABCD* has 8 "small sides" on its perimeter, so it has a perimeter of 8×1 = 8. (Don't count the "sides" *inside* square *ABCD*!)

    A) 8   B) 12   C) 16   D) 20

    30. A

The end of the contest ☞ **4**

Information & Solutions

Spring, 1993

Contest Information

4

- **Solutions** Turn the page for detailed contest solutions (written in the question boxes) and letter answers (written in the *Answer Column* to the right of each question).

- **Scores** Please remember that *this is a contest, not a test*—and there is no "passing" or "failing" score. Few students score as high as 24 points (80% correct). Students with half that, 12 points, *deserve commendation!*

- **Answers & Rating Scale** Turn to page 139 for the letter answers to each question and the rating scale for this contest.

1. $2 + 4 + 6 + 8 = 1+1 + 3+1 + 5+1 + 7+1 = 1+3+5+7 + 4.$

   A) 0   B) 1   C) 4   D) 9

   1. C

2. The thousands' digit is 2 and the tens' digit is 4. The sum is 6.

   A) 5   B) 6   C) 7   D) 8

   2. B

3. $(12 \times 7) - (12 + 12 + 12 + 12) = 83 - 48 = 36.$

   A) 36   B) 48   C) 72   D) 108

   3. A

4. The product of the number of sides of a rectangle and the number of sides of a triangle is $4 \times 3 = 12.$

   A) 9   B) 12   C) 16   D) 20

   4. B

5. $9 + 9 + 9 + 9 + 9 + 9 + 9 = $ seven 9's $= 9 \times 7.$

   A) 6   B) 7   C) 8   D) 9

   5. B

6. The number 1 billion is 1 thousand times 1 million.

   A) 1 thousand   B) 10 thousand
   C) 100 thousand   D) 1 billion

   6. D

7. I had 3 dozen socks in my drawer, which is 36 socks. When I lost 2 pairs, I lost 4 socks, so I had 32 socks left.

   A) 32   B) 34   C) 36   D) 40

   7. A

8. $1 + 10 + 100 + 1000 = 11 + 11$ hundred $= 1111.$

   A) 4   B) 1111   C) 1234   D) 4000

   8. B

9. If the wool from 1 sheep can make 4 sweaters, then you'll need $100 \div 4 = 25$ sheep to make 100 sweaters.

   A) 4   B) 5   C) 25   D) 400

   9. C

10. To make the product odd, both multipliers must be odd.

    A) 30×9 B) 3×90 C) 30×90 D) 3×9

    10. D

11. The number of months in a year minus the number of days in a week is $12 - 7 = 5.$

    A) 5   B) 7   C) 9   D) 19

    11. A

12. $5 + 50 + 500 = 555 = 5 \times 111.$

    A) 10   B) 100   C) 111   D) 550

    12. C

Go on to the next page ⟫ **4**

13. For a quarter (25¢), Pat can play a video game for 5 minutes. The number of 5-minute intervals in 1 hour is $60 \div 5 = 12$. A) 10 　　　B) 12 　　　C) 20 　　　D) 55	13. B
14. Since $100 \times 10 = 1000$, choice D is not equal to 10. A) $100 \div 10$ 　B) $10 \div 1$ 　　C) 10×1 　　D) 100×10	14. D
15. If 1 Earth year is equal to 3 years on the planet Trizone, then 12 Trizone years are the same as $12 \div 3 = 4$ Earth years. A) 4 　　　B) 10 　　　C) 36 　　　D) 48	15. A
16. 58 minutes before 6:10 P.M. is 5:10 P.M.+2 minutes = 5:12 P.M. A) 5:08 P.M. 　B) 5:12 P.M. 　C) 7:08 P.M. 　D) 7:12 P.M.	16. B
17. Otto needs 2 tentacles to juggle up to 3 balls. Using $8 = 4 \times 2$ tentacles, Otto can juggle up to $4 \times 3 = 12$ balls. A) 8 　　　B) 9 　　　C) 12 　　　D) 24	17. C
18. Each week has 7 days, so 52 weeks has $52 \times 7 = 364$ days. A) 364 　　B) 365 　　C) 366 　　D) 367	18. A
19. $99+101 + 99+101 + 99+101 = 200 + 200 + 200 = 600$. A) 200 　　B) 300 　　C) 600 　　D) 919	19. C
20. Today is Tues. 77 days ago was Tues. 76 days ago was Wed. A) Monday 　B) Tuesday 　C) Wednesday D) Thursday	20. C
21. The sides of a rectangle must be paired in length. Since the known sides are 1992, 1993, and 1993, the fourth side is 1992. A) 1992 　　B) 1993 　　C) 1994 　　D) 1995	21. A
22. $4 \times 10 \times 5 \times 10 \times 6 \times 10 = 4 \times 5 \times 6 \times 10 \times 10 \times 10 = 4 \times 5 \times 6 \times 1000$. A) 10 　　　B) 100 　　C) 456 　　D) 1000	22. D
23. $94 - 49 = 45$. A) 45 　　　B) 50 　　　C) 54 　　　D) 55	23. A

Go on to the next page Ⅲ➡ **4**

79

24. Scrooge told his secretary to double his yearly gift to the Bulldogs. His secretary said that his gift would still be the same amount after doubling. The only number equal to its double is 0.

   A) $0   B) $1   C) $10   D) $100

24.

A

25. In a leap year, there is 1 extra day, so there are 24 extra hours in a leap year.

   A) 1   B) 24   C) 48   D) 366

25.

B

26. Seventy-seven hundred = 7700 = 11×700.

   A) 70 × 70   B) 7 × 7000   C) 7 × 110   D) 11 × 700

26.

D

27. The *largest* divisor of $2 \times 3 \times 5 \times 7$ that is less than $2 \times 3 \times 5 \times 7$ is $3 \times 5 \times 7$, which we get by dropping the smallest factor.

   A) 357   B) 2357   C) 2 × 5 × 7   D) 3 × 5 × 7

27.

D

28. A *prime* number is a number greater than 1 whose only whole number factors are itself and 1. Of the numbers greater than 50, 51 = 3×17 and 52 = 2×26. The first prime is 53.

   A) 51   B) 52   C) 53   D) 59

28.

C

29. A bag contains 2 red, 2 blue, and 2 green marbles. Sue takes one marble at a time from this bag without looking. If she takes only 3 marbles, she could have taken 1 of each color. The very next marble must match one she already has.

   A) 2   B) 3   C) 4   D) 6

29.

C

30. Cut off a corner to get both a triangle and a 5-sided figure—a pentagon. Cut in half to get 2 rectangles.

   A) pentagon   B) triangle   C) rectangle   D) square

30.

D

The end of the contest 🖎 **4**

Information & Solutions

Spring, 1994

Contest Information

4

- **Solutions** Turn the page for detailed contest solutions (written in the question boxes) and letter answers (written in the *Answer Column* to the right of each question).

- **Scores** Please remember that *this is a contest, not a test*—and there is no "passing" or "failing" score. Few students score as high as 24 points (80% correct). Students with half that, 12 points, *deserve commendation!*

- **Answers & Rating Scale** Turn to page 140 for the letter answers to each question and the rating scale for this contest.

		Answer Column
1. $1 \times 9 \times 9 \times 4 = 9 \times 9 \times 4 = 81 \times 4 = 324$. A) 23 B) 36 C) 324 D) 1994 1994		1. C
2. 2 more than 4 more than $6 = 2 + (4 + 6) = 2 + 10 = 12$. A) 14 B) 12 C) 10 D) 8		2. B
3. $(77-66)+(55-44)+(33-22) + 11 = (11+11+11) + 11 = 11 + 33$. A) 0 B) 11 C) 22 D) 33		3. D
4. 1 dozen *pairs* of socks $= 12 \times 2$ socks $= 24$ socks. A) 6 B) 14 C) 24 D) 144		4. C
5. $999 + 111 = 1110$. A) 1000 B) 1010 C) 1110 D) 1111		5. C
6. $13 \times 13 \div 13 = 13 \times 1 = 13$. A) 169 B) 13 C) 1 D) 0		6. B
7. If today is Mon., yesterday was Sun. Two days before Sun. is Fri. A) Saturday B) Sunday C) Thursday D) Friday		7. D
8. $(1+2+3+4+5+6)-(1+3+5) = (2+4+6) = 12$. A) 8 B) 12 C) 21 D) 248		8. B
9. The ones' digit of $20+20+20$ is 0; but $14+20+24$ ends in an 8. A) $14 + 20 + 24$ B) $19 + 20 + 21$ C) $10 + 20 + 30$ D) $0 + 20 + 40$		9. A
10. $100 \times 0 \times$ anything $= 0 \times$ anything $= 0$. A) 0 B) 111 C) 100 101 D) 1 000 000		10. A
11. Wilt watches the weather in Waterville. He noticed that, in 1993, it rained on 1 of every 3 cloudy days in Waterville. If it rained on 36 days in Waterville in 1993, there were $3 \times 36 = 108$ cloudy days in Waterville in 1993. A) 12 B) 39 C) 72 D) 108		11. D
12. $22 \times 22 = 2 \times 11 \times 2 \times 11 = (11 \times 11) \times (2 \times 2) = (11 \times 11) \times 4$. A) 2 B) 4 C) 11 D) 121		12. B

Go on to the next page ⫸ **4**

13. I have 1 quarter, 1 dime, and 3 nickels. These 5 coins are worth the same amount as 25 + 10 + 15 = 50 pennies. A) 5 B) 40 C) 50 D) 113	13. C

14. A sentence is a *palindrome* if it reads the same forwards or backwards when we ignore both punctuation and capitalization. For example, the sentence "Was it a rat I saw?" is a palindrome. Of the following, only II and IV are palindromes.
   I. Gateman sees names, garageman sees name tag.
   II. A man, a plan, a canal—Panama!
   III. Tini saw drawer and reward was in it.
   IV. Ma is as selfless as I am.
 	
 A) 1   B) 2   C) 3   D) 4
	14.
	
	 B

15. $10+10+10 = (20+20+20)-(10+10+10) = 20+20+20 - 30.$ A) 3 B) 10 C) 20 D) 30	15. D
16. (# of sides of a rectangle) + (# of sides of a square) − (# of sides of a triangle) = 4 + 4 − 3 = 5. A) 4 B) 5 C) 7 D) 11	16. B
17. $77 + 77 + 77 = 7 \times 11 \times 3 = 21 \times 11.$ A) 6 B) 7 C) 11 D) 14	17. C
18. It takes Genie 20 minutes to teach his dog Moe to sit, 35 minutes to teach Moe to lie down, and 40 minutes to teach Moe to roll over—1 hr. 35 minutes in all. If Genie started at 1:40 P.M. and worked without stopping, Genie finished at 2:40 P.M. + 35 minutes = 3:15 P.M. A) 2:15 P.M. B) 2:35 P.M. C) 3:15 P.M. D) 3:35 P.M.	18. C
19. Of the following, only 111 111 is divisible by both 11 and 111. A) 111 B) 1111 C) 11 111 D) 111 111	19. D
20. 11 hundreds + 11 tens + 11 ones = 1100 + 110 + 11 = 1221. A) 1111 B) 1221 C) 11 110 D) 12 210	20. B
21. Since 42 is divisible by 6, the smallest whole number greater then 42 which is divisible by 6 is 42+6 = 48. A) 43 B) 45 C) 46 D) 48	21. D

Go on to the next page ⫸ **4**

22. Since Lee used all the letters of the alphabet that came after *b* but before *y*, Lee used all the letters except *a*, *b*, *y*, and *z*. Thus, Lee used 26−4 = 22 different letters.

A) 21   B) 22   C) 23   D) 24

22. B

23. In 1 234 567 ÷ 10, the remainder is the ones' digit, 7.

A) 7   B) 5   C) 3   D) 1

23. A

24. If the length of a diameter of a circle is 10, the length of a radius of this circle is 10 ÷ 2 = 5.

A) 5   B) 10   C) 15   D) 20

24. A

25. The sum of their three ages of is 26. Four years from now, each will be 4 years older, and their age sum will be 26+12 = 38.

A) 30   B) 33   C) 34   D) 38

25. D

26. Al has 5 quarters = $1.25. Bob also has $1.25, in dimes and pennies. To have as few coins as possible, Bob should have as many dimes as possible. 12 dimes + 5 pennies = 17 coins.

A) 13   B) 15   C) 17   D) 25

26. C

27. even number + odd number = odd number

A) odd   B) even   C) 1995   D) prime

27. A

28. The roller coaster holds 16 people every 3 minutes. The ferris wheel holds 9 people every 2 minutes. In 6 minutes, 2×16 = 32 people ride the roller coaster and 3×9 = 27 people ride the ferris wheel. Finally, 32 − 27 = 5.

A) 5   B) 14   C) 21   D) 30

28. A

29. In diagram II, there are 10 different rectangles: four 1×1's, three 1×2's, two 1×3's and one 1×4, for a total of 10 different rectangles in diagram II.

I
II

A) 4   B) 5   C) 7   D) 10

29. D

30. If 2+4+6+...+198+200 = 10 100, subtract 1 from each of the 100 numbers to get 1+3+5+...+197+199 = 10 100−100 = 10 000.

A) 5050   B) 9900   C) 10 000   D) 10 099

30. C

The end of the contest 4

84

Information & Solutions

Spring, 1995

Contest Information

4

- **Solutions** Turn the page for detailed contest solutions (written in the question boxes) and letter answers (written in the *Answer Column* to the right of each question).

- **Scores** Please remember that *this is a contest, not a test*—and there is no "passing" or "failing" score. Few students score as high as 24 points (80% correct). Students with half that, 12 points, *deserve commendation!*

- **Answers & Rating Scale** Turn to page 141 for the letter answers to each question and the rating scale for this contest.

1. $1 + 1 + 1 = 3$, so $1 + 1 + 1 + 5 = 8$.

   A) 1   B) 3   C) 5   D) 8

   1.
   C

2. The number of letters in the alphabet is 26,
   and $26 + 7 = 32$.

   A) 31   B) 32   C) 33   D) 182

   2.
   C

3. Both factors of 1 may be ignored.

   A) 405   B) 1995   C) 1997   D) 2996

   3.
   B

4. $40 \div 4 = 10$, with a remainder of 0.

   A) 0   B) 1   C) 3   D) 10

   4.
   A

5. $420 \div 8 = 52.5$, which *isn't* a whole number.

   A) 5   B) 6   C) 7   D) 8

   5.
   D

6. A bobsled can seat 7 kids, so $7 \times 77 =$
   539 kids can be seated on 77 bobsleds.

   A) 11 B) 84 C) 539 D) 777

   6.
   C

7. $2 \times 2 \times 2 \times 2 = 16 = 1 \times 1 \times 1 \times 1 \times 16$.

   A) 2 B) 4 C) 8 D) 16

   7.
   D

8. The hundreds' digit of 321, 3, plus the product of the tens' digit
   of 987, 8, and the ones' digit of 654, 4, is $3 + (8 \times 4) = 3 + 32 = 35$.

   A) 32   B) 35   C) 64   D) 96

   8.
   B

9. $(1994 - 1993) + (1995 - 1994) + (1996 - 1995) = 1 + 1 + 1 = 3$.

   A) 1   B) 3   C) 6   D) 1996

   9.
   B

10. In 30 days, the family of 60 mice eats
    60×2 kg $= 120$ kg of cheese; so each day
    the family eats $120 \div 30 = 4$ kg of cheese.

    A) 4 kg   B) 3 kg   C) 2 kg   D) 1 kg

    10.
    A

11. 1 decade is 10 years, so 100 decades is $100 \times 10 = 1000$ years.

    A) 10   B) 100   C) 110   D) 1000

    11.
    D

12. The sum is $4 + 6 + 8 + 10 = 28$.

    A) 14   B) 26   C) 28   D) 30

    12.
    C

Go on to the next page ▐▐▶ **4**

13. $7 \times 1 \times 1 \times 1 \times 1 \times 1 \times 1 \times 1 \times 7 = 7 \times 7 = 49.$ A) 717 B) 49 C) 21 D) 7	13. B
14. The difference between an even number and an odd number is always an odd number. A) 1 B) 9 C) 32 D) 77	14. C
15. Five less than six more than seven ears of corn is $(7+6) - 5 = 13-5 = 8$ ears of corn. A) 6 B) 7 C) 8 D) 9	15. C
16. $11+38 = 11+12+12+12+2 = 11:00 + 2$ hrs $= 1:00.$ A) 1 B) 2 C) 8 D) 12	16. A
17. Rita's rabbit hops twice as far as Larry's leapfrog. The rabbit jumps 2 m with each hop. If both pets take 3 hops, the rabbit goes 6 m and the frog goes 3 m. Finally, 6 m − 3 m = 3 m. A) 1 m B) 2 m C) 3 m D) 6 m	17. C
18. $4+4+4+4+4+4$ is six 4's $= 4 \times 6 = 4 \times (2+2+2).$ A) 2 B) 4 C) 6 D) 8	18. B
19. In Lenny's garden, only one 4-leaf clover grows for every ten 3-leaf clovers. The 22 clovers include two 4-leaf and twenty 3-leaf clovers, and $(2 \times 4) + (20 \times 3) = 8+60 = 68$ leaves. A) 66 B) 68 C) 88 D) 154	19. B
20. Since 1 *isn't* a prime, the product is $2 \times 3 \times 5 = 30.$ A) 6 B) 24 C) 30 D) 42	20. C
21. A square has 4 sides and a trapezoid has 4 sides. A) trapezoid B) pentagon C) triangle D) hexagon	21. A
22. Tarzan rode his elephant from 5:45 PM to 7:15 PM. That's 1 hour 30 minutes; so Tarzan rode his elephant for 90 minutes. A) 170 B) 150 C) 120 D) 90	22. D

Go on to the next page ⅢⅢ➡ **4**

23. I divide $1 \times 2 \times 3 \times 4 \times 5 \times 6 \times 7$ by a certain whole number. Then I continue dividing each new quotient by the same whole number until the remainder is no longer 0. There are four factors of 2 in $1 \times 2 \times 3 \times 4 \times 5 \times 6 \times 7 = 1 \times 2 \times 3 \times 2 \times 2 \times 5 \times 2 \times 3 \times 7$, so I can divide by 2, without remainder, the most number of times.

A) 2 B) 3 C) 4 D) 5

23.

A

24. $99 - 24 = 75$, and 15 nickels $= 75¢$, so it's worth 15 more nickels than a 24¢ ticket.

A) 13 B) 15 C) 25 D) 75

24.

B

25. Every whole number prime is divisible only by itself and 1.

A) even B) odd C) prime D) more than 2

25.

C

26. $0 \times 0 = 0$; $1 \times 1 = 1$; $2 \times 2 = 4$; $3 \times 3 = 9$; $4 \times 4 = 16$; $5 \times 5 = 25$; $6 \times 6 = 36$; $7 \times 7 = 49$; $8 \times 8 = 64$; $9 \times 9 = 81$.

A) 0 B) 5 C) 6 D) 7

26.

D

27. The 3rd number on my list is 5, and $(5+1)/2 = 3$, it's position on my list. In the same manner, the last number I listed was 1995; so there are $(1995+1)/2 = 998$ numbers on my list.

A) 997 B) 998 C) 999 D) 1995

27.

B

28. A month is called a *prime* month if its total number of days is prime. Since all of 1995's *prime* months have 31 days, there are 7 such months.

A) 0 B) 5 C) 6 D) 7

28.

D

29. Captain Quark runs twice as fast as Mr. Spoke. If Mr. Spoke can run it in 7 hrs. 10 mins. = 6 hrs. 70 mins., Captain Quark can run it in half that time, 3 hrs. 35 mins.

A) 3 hr 5 min B) 3 hr 35 min
C) 3 hr 55 min D) 14 hr 20 min

29.

B

30. Notice that $1001-999 = 2$ and $1001+999 = 2000$. Whenever the difference is 2 (or any even number), the *sum must be even.*

A) 1995 B) 1997 C) 1999 D) 2000

30.

D

The end of the contest ✍ **4**

88

Information & Solutions

Spring, 1996

Contest Information

4

- **Solutions** Turn the page for detailed contest solutions (written in the question boxes) and letter answers (written in the *Answer Column* to the right of each question).

- **Scores** Please remember that *this is a contest, not a test*—and there is no "passing" or "failing" score. Few students score as high as 24 points (80% correct). Students with half that, 12 points, *deserve commendation!*

- **Answers & Rating Scale** Turn to page 142 for the letter answers to each question and the rating scale for this contest.

Answer Column

1. $1+1 + 1+1 +...+ 1+1 = 5 \times (1+1) = 5 \times 2$.

   A) 5×2 B) 4×2 C) 2×2 D) 1×2

   1. A

2. Drop the "19," so $1999 - 1996 = 99 - 96$.

   A) 3   B) 6   C) 19   D) 96

   2. D

3. $99 + 111 = 210 = 200 + 10$.

   A) 0 B) 10 C) 11 D) 20

   3. B

4. The remainders are: A) 2 B) 3 C) 4 D) 5.

   A) $4002 \div 4$ B) $503 \div 5$ C) $604 \div 6$ D) $75 \div 7$

   4. A

5. Halfway up a hill, my friends and I stopped to pick berries. We picked 76 blackberries, 54 raspberries, 32 strawberries, and 1 gigantic blueberry. The number of berries we picked was $76 + 54 + 32 + 1 = 163$.

   A) 153 B) 161 C) 163 D) 165

   5. C

6. $(100 \div 10) \div 10 = 10 \div 10 = 1$.

   A) 0 B) 1 C) 10 D) 80

   6. B

7. Drop 1's: $3 \times 3 \times 3 = 9 \times 3$.

   A) 3 B) 9 C) 12 D) 27

   7. D

8. In the word divide, there are 3 vowels and 3 consonants.

   A) add   B) subtract   C) multiply   D) divide

   8. D

9. A crow earned a nickel for each hour it sang. If it earned 70¢ singing, it sang for $70 \div 5 = 14$ hours.

   A) 7   B) 12   C) 14   D) 35

   9. C

10. The product of three 5's $= 5 \times 5 \times 5 = 125$.

    A) 125 B) 50 C) 25 D) 15

    10. A

11. Two dozen pairs $= 24$ pairs $= 48$ pears.

    A) 12 B) 24 C) 40 D) 48

    11. D

12. Today is Tues. 14 days ago was Tues. 15 days ago was Mon.

    A) Saturday   B) Sunday   C) Monday   D) Wednesday

    12. C

Go on to the next page ⟩⟩⟩ **4**

90

13. The odd numbers between 20 and 30 are 21, 23, 25, 27, 29.		13.
A) 4 B) 5 C) 9 D) 10		B

14. Alice is only 30 cm tall. If eating all her veggies will make her 5 times as tall, Alice will grow to $5 \times 30 =$ 150 cm by eating all her veggies.

A) 6 B) 35 C) 50 D) 150

14.

D

15. $3 \times 77 \div 7 = 3 \times 11 = 33 = 66 \div 2.$

A) 2 B) 3 C) 6 D) 11

15.

A

16. To get the ones' digit, get the ones' digit of $3 \times 9 = 27.$

A) 0 B) 7 C) 8 D) 9

16.

B

17. If I counted 40 legs in a herd of sheep, then the herd had $40 \div 4 = 10$ sheep.

A) 10 B) 20
C) 36 D) 160

17.

A

18. Monday: 1 km, Tuesday: 2 km, Wednesday: 4 km, Thursday: 8 km, Friday: 16 km, and finally, Saturday: 32 km.

A) Friday B) Saturday C) Sunday D) Monday

18.

B

19. Every letter of the alphabet appeared 3 times in Di's alphabet soup. Di used the letter "l" twice in "cholesterol," so she has one "l" left. Her other word could *not* contain "l" twice, as does "multiply."

A) "add" B) "subtract"
C) "multiply" D) "divide"

19.

C

20. $1 \times 4 \times 16 = 16 \times 4 = (2 \times 8) \times 4.$

A) 1 B) 2 C) 4 D) 8

20.

C

21. A *Mega* comic costs as much as 3 *Multi* comics or 15¢ more than 2 *Multi* comics. Thus, the 3rd *Multi* comic costs 15¢. Since each *Multi* comic costs 15¢, a *Mega* comic costs 3 times as much, 45¢.

A) 5¢ B) 10¢ C) 30¢ D) 45¢

21.

D

Go on to the next page ⟶ **4**

22. Dale arrived 35 minutes before 2:22 P.M., so 18 minutes after Dale arrived was $35 - 18 = 17$ minutes before 2:22 P.M.

A) 1:29 P.M.   B) 1:47 P.M.   C) 2:05 P.M.   D) 2:40 P.M.

22.

C

23. Since I had $26, I could pay the $4 Carnival admission fee for myself and some friends. I was able to pay for myself and 5 friends and have $2 left.

A) 4   B) 5   C) 6   D) 7

23.

B

24. Mr. Sixpence counted to 600 by 6's. He started with 6. He counted $600 \div 6 = 100$ numbers, 99 of which were *less* than 600.

A) 98   B) 99   C) 100   D) 101

24.

B

25. The length of each side of the rectangle is an odd number. The rectangle's perimeter $= 2 \times (\text{length} + \text{width}) =$ an even number.

A) 15   B) 17   C) 19   D) 20

25.

D

26. There are 5 small triangles that contain one outer vertex and 5 larger triangles that contain 2 outer vertices.

A) 5   B) 9   C) 10   D) 15

26.

C

27. 1002 is most nearly doubled to 2001 if the order of its digits is reversed. (Note: 6003 is nearly halved when changed to 3006.)

A) 1002   B) 2003   C) 4668   D) 6003

27.

A

28. My chicken lays 5 eggs each week. It takes her $15 \times 12 \div 5 = 36$ weeks to lay 15 dozen eggs.

A) 18   B) 36   C) 60   D) 180

28.

B

29. $10+20+30+40 = (1+2+3+4) \times 10$.

A) 10   B) 40   C) 100   D) 10 000

29.

A

30. Rearrange: $0+1+2+3+\ldots+97+98 = (1+98)+(2+97)+(3+96)+ \ldots +(49+50) = 49 \times 99$. The ones' digit is a 1.

A) 9   B) 5   C) 1   D) 0

30.

C

The end of the contest ☞ **4**

5th Grade Solutions

1991-92 through 1995-96

Information & Solutions

Spring, 1992

Contest Information

5

- **Solutions** Turn the page for detailed contest solutions (written in the question boxes) and letter answers (written in the *Answer Column* to the right of each question).

- **Scores** Please remember that *this is a contest, not a test*—and there is no "passing" or "failing" score. Few students score as high as 24 points (80% correct). Students with half that, 12 points, *deserve commendation!*

- **Answers & Rating Scale** Turn to page 143 for the letter answers to each question and the rating scale for this contest.

1991-92 5TH GRADE CONTEST SOLUTIONS

1. $(1992 + 1992) \times (1992 - 1992) = (1992+1992) \times 0 = 0.$

   A) 0   B) 1   C) 1992   D) 3984

2. 50+51 is more than 50+50, so 50+51 is more than 100.

   A) 47 + 48   B) 50 + 51   C) 49 + 50   D) 48 + 49

3. $703 + 307 = 700+300 + 3+7 = 1000 + 10 = 1010.$

   A) 110   B) 1010   C) 1100   D) 10010

4. The product of the number of days in a week and the number of months in a year is $7 \times 12 = 84.$

   A) 5   B) 19   C) 60   D) 84

5. $(11 + 22 + 33) \div (1 + 2 + 3) = 66 \div 6 = 11.$

   A) 10   B) 11   C) 30   D) 33

6. The whole number factors of 4 are 1, 2, and 4. For 5, they're 1 and 5. For 9, they're 1, 3, and 9. For 8, they're 1, 2, 4, and 8.

   A) 4   B) 5   C) 8   D) 9

7. Jack has seven dozen pencils and Jill has eight dozen pencils. Jill has one dozen more than Jack, and one dozen is 12.

   A) 1   B) 12   C) 24   D) 96

8. Odd + even is odd, so 949 + 494 won't have an even sum.

   A) 977 + 111   B) 282 + 828   C) 189 + 891   D) 949 + 494

9. The sum of 7 numbers is 567. Their average is $567 \div 7 = 81.$

   A) 81   B) 88   C) 91   D) 98

10. $11-10+12-10+13-10+14-10+15-10 = 11+12+13+14+15-50.$

    A) 10   B) 16   C) 50   D) 100

11. Jan+Feb+Mar=31+(28 or 29)+31=90 or 91. Day 100 is in Apr.

    A) March   B) April   C) May   D) June

Go on to the next page ⫸ **5**

1991-92 5TH GRADE CONTEST SOLUTIONS

		Answer Column

12. $1\times2\times3\times4\times5\times6 = (1\times2)\times(3\times4)\times(5\times6) = 2\times12\times30$.

    A) 18   B) 20   C) 24   D) 30

12.
D

13. Since 4 goes into 36 exactly 9 times, 37 will leave a remainder of 1 when divided by 4.

    A) 37   B) 35   C) 31   D) 27

13.
A

14. $1 + 22 + 333 + 4444 = 23 + 333 + 4444 = 356 + 4444 = 4800$.

    A) 4790   B) 4800   C) 5000   D) 5100

14.
B

15. I own 1 white, 2 black, and 3 brown pigs. The white pig is the *only* one which is *not* the same color as one or more of the other pigs, so it's the only one who could make that statement.

    A) 3   B) 4   C) 5   D) 6

15.
C

16. Since one-half year is 6 months, and 9 years is $9\times12 = 108$ months, nine and one-half years $= 6 + 108 = 114$ months.

    A) 95   B) 104   C) 108   D) 114

16.
D

17. The product $10\times10\times10\times10\times10\times10$ is 1 000 000, and this number has 7 digits.

    A) 6   B) 7   C) 10   D) 1 000 000

17.
B

18. As shown, the line can intersect 0, 1 or 2 times.

    A) 3   B) 2   C) 1   D) 0

18.
A

19. Ann *makes* 5 out of every 6 shots she tries. If she tries 30 times, it's like 5 rounds of 6 shots. She'll *make* $5\times5 = 25$ shots.

    A) 20   B) 24   C) 25   D) 29

19.
C

20. One thousand thousands is equal to 1 million.

    A) 10×10 B) 100×100 C) 1000×100 D) 1000×1000

20.
D

21. If he left at 7:20 A.M., he'd have 40 minutes to get to school on time. Leaving at 7:21 A.M. leaves 1 minute less than that.

    A) 21   B) 29   C) 39   D) 79

21.
C

Go on to the next page ⫸ **5**

22. 300 and 15 are both divisible by 15, so 300+15 is divisible by 15.

22.

C

A) 115　　　B) 215　　　C) 315　　　D) 415

23. Any two consecutive whole numbers are 1 apart, so the difference between any two such numbers is always 1.

23.

A

A) 1　　　B) 2　　　C) 996　　　D) 1992

24. If two *different* whole numbers are both less than 10, they *could* be 0 and 1. In such a case, their product would equal $0 \times 1 = 0$.

24.

A

A) 0　　　B) 1　　　C) 100　　　D) 101

25. Divide out the common numbers. The number remaining is 27.

25.

D

A) 1　　　B) 4　　　C) 5　　　D) 27

26. The smallest odd number greater than 399 is 401. When 401 is divided by 10, the remainder is 1.

26.

B

A) 0　　　B) 1　　　C) 3　　　D) 9

27. In rectangle *ABCD*, the side *opposite* $\overline{BD}$ is the segment parallel to $\overline{BD}$.

27.

D

A) $\overline{AB}$　　　B) $\overline{CD}$　　　C) $\overline{BC}$　　　D) $\overline{AC}$

28. Every prime greater than 2 is odd, so its ones' digit is odd.

28.

C

A) 1　　　B) 3　　　C) odd　　　D) even

29. 3 gremlins = 5 gizmos; $3 \times 15 = 45$ gremlins = $5 \times 15 = 75$ gizmos.

29.

D

A) 27　　　B) 30　　　C) 47　　　D) 75

30. A whole number is a *perfect square* if it is the product of two equal whole numbers. Thus, 1×1 and 2×2 and 3×3 and 4×4 are perfect squares. Continue until the product is bigger than 1000: $30 \times 30 = 900$; $31 \times 31 = 961$; $32 \times 32 = 1024$ (too big).

30.

B

A) 30　　　B) 31　　　C) 32　　　D) 33

The end of the contest ✍ **5**

Information & Solutions

Spring, 1993

Contest Information

5

- **Solutions** Turn the page for detailed contest solutions (written in the question boxes) and letter answers (written in the *Answer Column* to the right of each question).

- **Scores** Please remember that *this is a contest, not a test*—and there is no "passing" or "failing" score. Few students score as high as 24 points (80% correct). Students with half that, 12 points, *deserve commendation!*

- **Answers & Rating Scale** Turn to page 144 for the letter answers to each question and the rating scale for this contest.

1. $11+12+13 = 10+1 + 11+1 + 12+1 = 10+11+12 + 1+1+1.$

   A) 0   B) 1   C) 3   D) 6

2. 8 hundreds + 17 tens = $800 + 170 = 970.$

   A) 8170   B) 870   C) 817   D) 970

3. After each person passes 2 pears to the person on the right, each person will have the original number of pears, 4.

   A) 2 pears   B) 4 pears   C) 6 pears   D) 12 pears

4. $32 \div 2 = 16 = 2 \times 8.$

   A) 4   B) 8   C) 16   D) 32

5. A certain bird flies south. If it flies 120 km each day and it flies 3000 km in all, it flies for $3000 \div 120 = 25$ days.

   A) 120   B) 50   C) 25   D) 15

6. $(1 \times 2 \times 3 \times 4 \times 5) \div 10 = 120 \div 10 = 12.$

   A) 7   B) 12   C) 23   D) 24

7. The difference between two numbers is 333. If the smaller number is 321, the larger number is $321 + 333 = 654.$

   A) 666   B) 654   C) 456   D) 345

8. $10 + 100 + 1000 = 1110 = 10 \times 111.$

   A) 100   B) 110   C) 111   D) 1000

9. The quotient $128 \div 128 = 1$, which is an odd number.

   A) $128 \div 128$ B) $128 \div 64$ C) $128 \div 32$ D) $128 \div 16$

10. (4 sides of a square) + (5 sides of a pentagon) − (6 sides of a hexagon) = (3 sides of a triangle).

    A) a triangle   B) a rectangle   C) a pentagon   D) an octagon

11. $(7 \times 15) - (7 + 14 + 21 + 28) = 7 \times 15 - 70 = 35 = 7 \times 5.$

    A) 0   B) 1   C) 3   D) 5

12. Mary can buy 5 candy bars for 60¢. The cost for 10 candy bars would be twice 60¢ = $1.20.

    A) 12¢   B) 65¢   C) $1.20   D) $3.00

Go on to the next page ⮞ **5**

13. The average of 7, 7, 7, 7, 7, 7, and 21 is $(42+21) \div 7 = 63 \div 7 = 9$	13.	C
A) 7 B) 8 C) 9 D) 14		
14. The product $2 \times 2 \times 2 \times 2 \times 2 \times 2 \times 5 \times 5 \times 5 \times 5 \times 5 \times 5$ is $10 \times 10 \times 10 \times 10 \times 10 \times 10 = 1\,000\,000$, a 7-digit number.	14.	B
A) 6 B) 7 C) 10 D) 12		
15. The sum of the ten-thousands' digit and the hundreds' digit of $1\,234\,567$ is $3 + 5 = 8$.	15.	C
A) 6 B) 7 C) 8 D) 9		
16. $341 - 143 = 198$.	16.	A
A) 198 B) 208 C) 218 D) 484		
17. The remainder is 6 since adding 1 makes the result divisible by 7.	17.	D
A) 0 B) 1 C) 2 D) 6		
18. 96¢ is closer to $1 than 85¢ or $1.20 or $1.25.	18.	A
A) 96 pennies B) 17 nickels C) 12 dimes D) 5 quarters		
19. 2 hours 57 minutes *before* 12:10 A.M. is 9:10 A.M. + 3 minutes.	19.	A
A) 9:13 P.M. B) 10:07 P.M. C) 10:13 P.M. D) 3:07 A.M.		
20. $10 \times 20 \times 30 = 1 \times 2 \times 3 \times 10 \times 10 \times 10 = 6 \times 1000$.	20.	D
A) 10 B) 100 C) 500 D) 1000		
21. As shown, ABCD is a rectangle. A pair of parallel sides would be any pair of opposite sides.	21.	C
A) $\overline{AB}, \overline{BC}$ B) $\overline{DA}, \overline{AB}$ C) $\overline{AB}, \overline{CD}$ D) $\overline{DC}, \overline{BC}$		
22. I am thinking of two numbers. The first number is 30 less than twice the second number. If the second number is 16, then the first is $2 \times 16 - 30 = 32 - 30 = 2$, and the sum is $16 + 2 = 18$.	22.	B
A) 2 B) 18 C) 46 D) 48		
23. A polygon must have 3 or more sides.	23.	A
A) 2 B) 3 C) 7 D) 1993		

Go on to the next page ⟱ **5**

24. The average of my three test grades is 60. If I get 100 on my next test, my average will be $(60+60+60+100) \div 4 = 280 \div 4 = 70$. A) 80 B) 75 C) 70 D) 65	24. C
25. To get the ones' digit multiply just the 7's: $7 \times 7 \times 7$ ends in 3. A) 1 B) 3 C) 7 D) 9	25. B
26. The binary tree grows on the Island of Twos. It has 2 branches when it is 1 year old. It doubles the number of branches each year, so it has 4 branches at age 2, it has 8 branches at age 3, it has 16 branches at age 4, and it has 32 branches at age 5. A) 5 B) 10 C) 16 D) 32	26. D
27. To get the greatest *common* divisor, use all *common* prime factors. A) $2 \times 3 \times 5$ B) 235 C) 7×11 D) $2 \times 3 \times 5 \times 7 \times 11$	27. A
28. If you cut a triangular sheet of paper along a straight line, you cannot get a square: that would require *at least* two cuts. A) an acute triangle B) a right triangle C) a trapezoid D) a square	28. D
29. When you add the length and width together, you'll get an even number. When you double this, the result must be divisible by 4. A) 16 B) 136 C) 180 D) 246	29. D
30. Each of the six Acrobatic Acropolis Brothers is exactly 180 cm tall. When one stands on any brother's shoulders, together they are 330 cm tall. Thus, each additional brother adds 150 cm to the height. For 6 brothers, the total height is $180 \text{ cm} + 5 \times 150 \text{ cm} = 930 \text{ cm}$. A) 900 cm B) 930 cm C) 960 cm D) 990 cm	30. B

The end of the contest ✍ **5**

Information & Solutions

Spring, 1994

Contest Information

5

- **Solutions** Turn the page for detailed contest solutions (written in the question boxes) and letter answers (written in the *Answer Column* to the right of each question).

- **Scores** Please remember that *this is a contest, not a test*—and there is no "passing" or "failing" score. Few students score as high as 24 points (80% correct). Students with half that, 12 points, *deserve commendation!*

- **Answers & Rating Scale** Turn to page 145 for the letter answers to each question and the rating scale for this contest.

1. $22 + 33 + 44 = 99 = 3 \times 33$.

   A) 11   B) 33   C) 99   D) 297

   1. B

2. Eight eighty-eights equals $88 \times 8 = 704$.

   A) 98   B) 704   C) 888   D) 7040

   2. B

3. Ignoring 1's, $1 \times 2 \times 1 \times 3 \times 1 \times 4 \times 1 \times 5 = 2 \times 3 \times 4 \times 5 = 2 \times 3 \times 4 \times 5 \times 1$.

   A) 1   B) 4   C) 6   D) 8

   3. A

4. $10100 \div 100$ leaves remainder 0, so $10101 \div 100$ leaves remainder 1.

   A) 0   B) 1   C) 2   D) 3

   4. B

5. $19+29+39+1+1+1 = 19+1 + 29+1 + 39+1 = 20+30+40+0$.

   A) 0   B) 1   C) 3   D) 6

   5. A

6. The 4940 quarters are worth $\$(4940 \div 4) = \$1235$.

   A) \$1235   B) \$2470

   C) \$4940   D) \$19760

   6. A

7. $32 - 16 + 16 - 8 + 8 - 4 + 4 - 2 = 32 - 2 = 30$.

   A) 34   B) 32   C) 30   D) 28

   7. C

8. Since $1 \div 1 = 1$, but $1 - 1 = 0$, the answer is D.

   A) 1×1 B) $2 \div 2$ C) $1 \times 1 \div 1$ D) $1 - 1$

   8. D

9. The average of 7, 8, 9, 10, 11, 12, 13 is the middle number, 10.

   A) 7   B) 10   C) 17   D) 70

   9. B

10. In Weird Al's collection of 40 spiders, each spider has 8 legs. All together, Weird Al has $8 \times 40 = 320$ spider legs.

    A) 5   B) 48   C) 160   D) 320

    10. D

11. 125 days is about 4 months + 1 week, so it will be late August.

    A) June   B) July   C) August   D) September

    11. C

12. Since $60 \div (2+3) = 60 \div 5 = 12$, we must have added together 12 2's and 12 3's to get 60.

    A) 5   B) 10   C) 12   D) 20

    12. C

13. $(1 + 1) \times (2 + 2) = 2 \times 4 = 8 = 2 + 6$.

    A) 1   B) 4   C) 6   D) 8

    13. C

Go on to the next page ▐▐▶ **5**

14. Mary is 10 years old. Since Mary is 3 years older than Mark, Mark is 7. Since John is twice as old as Mary, John is 20. Therefore, John is 13 years older than Mark. A) 7 B) 10 C) 13 D) 20	14. C
15. If, upon division by 10, the quotient is 99 and the remainder is 9, then the original number is $(99 \times 10) + 9 = 990 + 9 = 999$. A) 11 B) 90 C) 108 D) 999	15. D
16. The number of hours in 3 full days is $3 \times 24 = 72$. The number of minutes in one hour is 60, and $72 - 60 = 12$. A) 12 B) 36 C) 57 D) 4320	16. A
17. The numbers 11, 22, 33, 44, 55, 66, 77, 88, 99 are divisible by 11. A) 8 B) 9 C) 10 D) 11	17. B
18. Round 126 to the nearest 10 to get 130. Multiply by 2 to get 260. Round 260 to the nearest hundred to get 300. A) 200 B) 240 C) 260 D) 300	18. D
19. When Dad won \$9889 in the lottery, Mom won \$6776! Dad won $\$9889 - \$6776 = \$3113$ more than Mom in this lottery. A) \$3113 B) \$3131 C) \$3223 D) \$16 665	19. A
20. Paula's school usually starts at 8:05 A.M. Tomorrow she must be at school 50 minutes early. Since one hour early would be 7:05 A.M., she can arrive 10 minutes later, at 7:15 A.M. A) 6:55 A.M. B) 7:05 A.M. C) 7:15 A.M. D) 7:55 A.M.	20. C
21. I own 5 plastic dinosaurs, and each has 4 legs. If I paint 3 stripes on each dinosaur leg, then I painted $5 \times 4 \times 3 = 60$ stripes all together. A) 12 B) 15 C) 20 D) 60	21. D
22. Bubble gum comes in packs of 5 pieces of gum. To buy gum for herself and her 7 friends (8 people), so each person can have at least 2 pieces of gum, Robin needs at least 16 pieces of gum. Since 3 packs have 15 pieces, she'll need at least 4 packs of gum. A) 2 B) 3 C) 4 D) 5	22. C

Go on to the next page ▐▶ **5**

23. A right triangle cannot have any angle bigger than 90°, so 120° cannot be the measure of an angle in a right triangle.

    A) 30°   B) 60°   C) 90°   D) 120°

    23.

    D

24. Gil & Jill rode 3 times each, for a total of 6 times. Bill the Thrill rode 9 times. They rode 15 times all together, so the average number of rides they took was 15÷3 = 5.

    A) 4   B) 5
    C) 6   D) 12

    24.

    B

25. For any whole number N, let $\#N$ be the number of letters it takes to write N as an English word. For example, $\#18 = 8$, since the word "**eighteen**" has 8 letters. The **only** whole number N for which $\#N = N$ is $N = 4$, since "**four**" has 4 letters.

    A) 0   B) 1   C) 2   D) 4

    25.

    B

26. The greatest number of even numbers occurs when the numbers are furthest apart. The greatest difference is $141-25 = 116$.

    A) 25 and 141   B) 137 and 245 C) 183 and 297 D) 249 and 363

    26.

    A

27. The plant grows 1 leaf the first month, then triples its leaves each month. Its number of leaves is 1 after 1 month, 3 after 2 months, 9 after 3 months, 27 after 4 months, 81 after 5 months. It takes 6 months before it has more than 90 leaves.

    A) 5   B) 6   C) 30   D) 31

    27.

    B

28. To get the right-most digit, first multiply the 2 and the 5. This product, 10, ends in a 0, so the whole product ends in 0.

    A) 0   B) 1   C) 4   D) 6

    28.

    A

29. $1×2×3×4×5×6×7×8×9×10 = 3628800$. There are 10 *additional* 0's in $10×20×30×40×50×60×70×80×90×100$. Add 2 (the number of 0's in $3\,628\,800$) to 10 to get the answer, $10 + 2 = 12$.

    A) 2   B) 10   C) 12   D) 13

    29.

    C

30. $200-100 + \ldots + 101-1 = 100+ \ldots +100$, a total of 100 times.

    A) 99   B) 100   C) 199   D) 200

    30.

    B

The end of the contest ✍ **5**

Information & Solutions

Spring, 1995

Contest Information

5

- **Solutions** Turn the page for detailed contest solutions (written in the question boxes) and letter answers (written in the *Answer Column* to the right of each question).

- **Scores** Please remember that *this is a contest, not a test*—and there is no "passing" or "failing" score. Few students score as high as 24 points (80% correct). Students with half that, 12 points, *deserve commendation!*

- **Answers & Rating Scale** Turn to page 146 for the letter answers to each question and the rating scale for this contest.

1. $18 = 14 + 4$, and 4 days from Tues. is Sat.
   A) Wed. B) Thurs. C) Fri. D) Sat.

   1. D

2. Ignoring 1's, $11 \times 11 \times 11 = 11 \times 121$
   A) 3 B) 11 C) 33 D) 121

   2. D

3. If there are 5 vowels in the English alphabet and the other letters are all consonants, there are $26 - 5 = 21$ consonants.
   A) 21 B) 22 C) 25 D) 26

   3. A

4. $600 - [(98+102) + (99+101) + 100] = 600 - 500 = 100$.
   A) 0 B) 80 C) 100 D) 904

   4. C

5. I paid with 5 quarters, 5 dimes, and 5 pennies, worth $1.80. I could have paid with $180 \div 5 = 36$ nickels.
   A) 8 B) 15 C) 28 D) 36

   5. D

6. Factor out a 4: $4+8+12+16 = (1+2+3+4) \times 4$.
   A) 4 B) 16 C) 18 D) 256

   6. A

7. 111 more than $99 = 99 + 111 = 210$.
   A) 12 B) 110 C) 200 D) 210

   7. D

8. The 4 remainders of 1 add to another 4; so the remainder is 0.
   A) 0 B) 1 C) 2 D) 3

   8. A

9. $(333+333)+(333+333)+(333+333) = 666+666+666 = 666 \times 3$.
   A) 1 B) 2 C) 3 D) 6

   9. C

10. Since 1 *isn't* a prime, the product is $2 \times 3 \times 5 = 30$.
    A) 6 B) 24 C) 30 D) 105

    10. C

11. In a dog race, my dog ran after a mail truck and finished 7th best (which was also 7th from last). There were 6 dogs ahead of my dog and 6 dogs behind, plus my dog, for a total of 13 dogs in the race.
    A) 7 B) 13 C) 14 D) 15

    11. B

12. A polygon has straight sides, so a circle isn't a polygon.
    A) a square B) a circle C) a triangle D) a hexagon

    12. B

Go on to the next page ▐▐▶ **5**

13. Three kids rubbed a magic lamp an average of 13 times each. If one kid rubbed the lamp 13 times, the other two kids still averaged 13 rubs each, which is *not* the average in choice A.
    A) 10 and 14   B) 11 and 15
    C) 0 and 26   D) 9 and 17

13.

A

14. There's a factor of 0, so $1000\times100\times10\times1\times0 = 0$.
    A) 0   B) 1   C) 1111   D) 1000000

14.
A

15. The product of the three odd numbers which are greater than 3 and less than 11 is $5\times7\times9 = 315$.
    A) 21   B) 35   C) 105   D) 315

15.
D

16. From 5:59 P.M. to 6:59 P.M. is 60 minutes. It's 2 minutes more from 6:59 to 7:01.
    A) 52   B) 62   C) 102   D) 122

16.
B

17. Of the following, the one nearest in value to $10\times10 = 100$ is $9\times11 = 99$.
    A) 9×9 B) 9×10 C) 9×11 D) 10×11

17.
C

18. $10\times10 + 9\times9 + 8\times8 = 100+81+64 = 245$.
    A) 145   B) 243   C) 245   D) 720

18.
C

19. The tens' digit is 8, and the product of the ten-thousands' and hundreds' digits is $5\times7 = 35$. The sum is $8+35 = 43$.
    A) 20   B) 43   C) 47   D) 50

19.
B

20. I sent half the books on Monday, 8 more on Tuesday, and the final 2 on Wednesday. I must have sent $8+2 = 10$ on Monday, so I shipped 20 books altogether.
    A) 16   B) 18   C) 20   D) 22

20.

C

21. In 2 hrs, there are $2\times60\times60 = 7200$ seconds.
    A) 120   B) 720   C) 3600   D) 7200

21.
D

22. Look at $333333 \div 9$ and $333333333 \div 9$ to see the pattern.
    A) 37373737   B) 37037037037037
    C) 370370370370370   D) 37373737373737

22.

B

Go on to the next page ⫸ **5**

23. See the picture. They can cross at most 8 times.

A) 2   B) 4   C) 6   D) 8

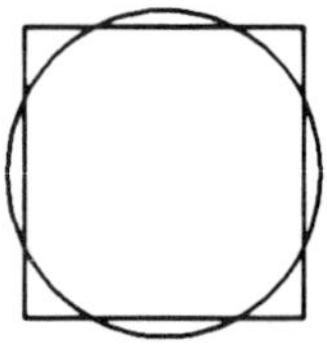

23.
D

24. $(100 - 99) \times \ldots \times (2 - 1) = 1 \times \ldots \times 1 = 1.$

A) 1   B) 5   C) 100   D) 200

24.
A

25. Since the sum of the lengths of the 5 sides is 35, each side has a length of $35 \div 5 = 7$; and the perimeter of the triangle is $3 \times 7 = 21$.

A) 7   B) 15   C) 21   D) 28

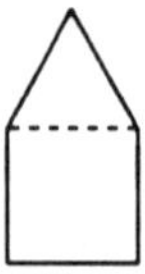

25.
C

26. If 192 is divided by 3, the quotient is 64. When you divide out all odd factors, only 1 and (lots of) 2's can remain as factors.

A) 23   B) 36   C) 48   D) 64

26.
D

27. A magic carpet ride costs 25¢ per minute with a rental phone and 10¢ per minute without one. For $2, I'd fly 8 minutes with and 20 minutes without the phone; and $20 - 8 = 12$.

A) 8   B) 12
C) 13   D) 20

27.
B

28. The perimeter of the larger of two squares is 8 times the perimeter of the smaller. As seen in the diagram, we can fit 64 small squares into the large square.

A) 4   B) 8   C) 16   D) 64

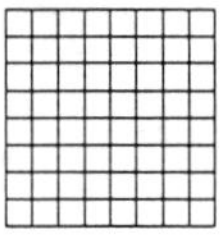

28.
D

29. The product contains $2 \times 5 = 10$ as a factor, so its 1's digit is 0.

A) 0   B) 1   C) 4   D) 7

29.
A

30. The number could be ✿999999 or 9*99999 or 99*9999 or 999*999 or 9999*99 or 99999*9 or 999999*. The single ✿ could be any of the 8 digits, 1–8. The six *'s could be any of the 9 digits, 0–8. All together, there are $8 + (6 \times 9) = 62$ different numbers.

A) 7   B) 9   C) 62   D) 63

30.
C

The end of the contest ☝ **5**

Information & Solutions

Spring, 1996

Contest Information

5

- **Solutions** Turn the page for detailed contest solutions (written in the question boxes) and letter answers (written in the *Answer Column* to the right of each question).

- **Scores** Please remember that *this is a contest, not a test*—and there is no "passing" or "failing" score. Few students score as high as 24 points (80% correct). Students with half that, 12 points, *deserve commendation!*

- **Answers & Rating Scale** Turn to page 147 for the letter answers to each question and the rating scale for this contest.

1. Rearranging: $11-9 + \ldots + 11-9 = 2+ \ldots +2 = 2\times 6 = 12.$ A) 2 B) 6 C) 12 D) 102	1. C
2. Since $44 \div 8$ is between 5 and 6, if each pizza is cut into 8 slices, then 6 pizzas will provide 44 slices with 4 slices left over. A) 2 B) 4 C) 5 D) 6	2. D
3. $1\times 5\times 1\times 5\times 1\times 5 = 5\times 5\times 5 = 125.$ A) 15 B) 18 C) 45 D) 125	3. D
4. A pentagon has 5 sides, one more side than a square. A) a circle B) a pentagon C) a triangle D) a rectangle	4. B
5. If a pat on the back costs 25¢, I can buy 3 pats for 75¢, the value of 5 nickels + 5 dimes. A) 2 B) 3 C) 4 D) 5	5. B
6. The quotients are: A) 1 B) 4 C) 2 D) 16 A) $64 \div 64$ B) $64 \div 16$ C) $16 \div 8$ D) $16 \div 1$	6. A
7. The greatest common divisors of the pairs below are: A) 1 B) 2 C) 2 D) 2. A) 1 & 2 B) 2 & 4 C) 4 & 6 D) 6 & 8	7. A
8. D, the sum of only even numbers, must be an even number. A) $1 + 2 + 4 + 8 + 16$ B) $1 + 2 + 1 + 2 + 1$ C) $1 + 2 + 3 + 4 + 5$ D) $2 + 4 + 6 + 8 + 10$	8. D
9. Lisa mailed some postcards to 10 friends while she was on vacation. She sent 3 of them 1 postcard each, and 7 of them 2 postcards each for a total of $3\times 1 + 7\times 2 = 3 + 14 = 17$ postcards in all. A) 13 B) 14 C) 17 D) 23	9. C
10. $(77\,777\,777\,777 +7)\div 7 = 11\,111\,111\,111+1.$ A) 11 111 111 112 B) 11 111 111 111 C) 11 111 111 110 D) 77 777 777 770	10. A
11. $4\times 12 = 48$ and $7\times 12 = 84.$ The greatest common factor is 12. A) 4 B) 6 C) 12 D) 24	11. C

Go on to the next page ▐▌▶ **5**

12. A race began at 3:43 P.M. and ended
2 hrs 14 minutes later, at 5:57 P.M.
Halftime was 3:43 + 1 hr 7 mins.

A) 4:20   B) 4:30   C) 4:50   D) 5:00

12.
C

13. Since 4 is 3 more than 1, one
number is 1, the other number
is 8 − 1 = 7, and 3 + 7 = 10.

A) 11   B) 10   C) 7   D) 4

13.
B

14. Since $7 \times 29 = 203$ and $7 \times 28 = 196$, which is less than 200, the
smallest number whose product with 7 is more than 200 is 29.

A) 30   B) 29   C) 28   D) 27

14.
B

15. When I subtract 20 from 4 times my number, the result is 100.
Reversing procedures: add 20 to 100, then divide by 4 to get 30.

A) 120   B) 80   C) 40   D) 30

15.
D

16. Paul read 20 short stories, each 10 pages long.
Anne read 10 books, each 50 pages
long. Anne read 500 − 200 =
300 more pages than Paul.

A) 30   B) 40   C) 300   D) 400

16.

C

17. 8888 + 220 = 9108 = 8000 + 1108.

A) 118   B) 888   C) 1008   D) 1108

17.
D

18. To get the largest quotient, divide by the smallest number.

A) $4800 \div 2$ B) $4800 \div 3$ C) $4800 \div 4$ D) $4800 \div 5$

18.
A

19. My family can eat 40 sandwiches
every 3 days. In 12 days, we can eat
$(12 \div 3) \times 40 = 4 \times 40 = 160$ sandwiches.

A) 160   B) 120   C) 80   D) 60

19.

A

20. $10 \times (2 \times 10 \times 3 \times 10) = 10 \times (20 \times 30)$.

A) 2×3 B) 5×10
C) 20×3 D) 20×30

20.

D

21. As shown below, only 5 *cannot* be written as the sum
of three different whole numbers, each greater than 0.

A) 5   B) $6 = 1+2+3$ C) $7 = 1+2+4$ D) $8 = 1+2+5 = 1+3+4$

21.
A

Go on to the next page ⮕ **5**

22. If a camera takes 64 pictures every second, in 10 minutes it will take $10 \times 60 \times 64 = 64 \times 600$ pictures. A) 10×60 B) 64×10 C) 64×60 D) 64×600		22. D
23. First, Captain Ahab sailed 200 km across the Moby Sea. Then, he sailed 600 km to Oyster Island. Altogether, he sailed $200 + 600 = 800$ km. A) 203 B) 600 C) 800 D) 1200		23. C
24. Each side of a square is 2. The perimeter uses 8 of these sides, and $8 \times 2 = 16$. A) 8 B) 16 C) 20 D) 24		24. B
25. Since 7 leaves a remainder of 6 when divided into 1000, every number Lucky counts also leaves a remainder of 6 when divided by 7. A) 0 B) 1 C) 3 D) 6		25. D
26. $111 \div 4 = 27$, with remainder 3, so the quotient times remainder $= 27 \times 3 = 81$. A) 1 B) 30 C) 81 D) 111		26. C
27. The product includes the factor $5 \times 2 = 10$, so the ones' digit is 0. A) 0 B) 1 C) 2 D) 5		27. A
28. Since 1 two-liter bottle costs the same as 5 cans *or* 60¢ more than 3 cans, 2 cans cost 60¢, and 1 can costs 30¢. Finally, the bottle costs as much as 5 cans, $1.50. A) $1.00 B) $1.20 C) $1.50 D) $1.80		28. C
29. If the sum of consecutive odd numbers is 1000, the smaller number is 1 less than half $= 500 - 1$. A) 1 B) 499 C) 500 D) 999		29. B
30. Rearrange: $1 + 99 + 2 + 98 + \ldots + 49 + 51 + 50 + 50 = 100 \times 50$. A) 500 B) 5000 C) 5050 D) 5100		30. B

The end of the contest 👈 **5**

114

6th Grade Solutions

1991-92 through 1995-96

Information & Solutions

Tuesday, March 10, 1992

Contest Information

6

- **Solutions** Turn the page for detailed contest solutions (written in the question boxes) and letter answers (written in the *Answers* column to the right of each question).

- **Scores** Please remember that *this is a contest, not a test*—and there is no "passing" or "failing" score. Few students score as high as 30 points (75% correct). Students with half that, 15 points, *deserve commendation!*

- **Answers & Rating Scale** Turn to page 148 for the letter answers to each question and the rating scale for this contest.

1. The only missing month is February. The sum will be either $365 - 28$ or (in leap years) $366 - 29$. *Both* are equal to 337. A) 334 B) 335 C) 336 D) 337	1. D
2. Since 5 divides 1000, 900, and 90, the remainder is 2. A) 1 B) 2 C) 3 D) 4	2. B
3. $(100-1)+(101-2)+(102-3)+(103-4) = 99+99+99+99 = 400-4$. A) 0 B) 3 C) 4 D) 10	3. C
4. An even number has a factor of 2. Such a number, when multiplied by 5, will have a factor of 10. Its ones' digit will be 0. A) 0 B) 1 C) 2 D) 5	4. A
5. $10^3+(10^3-10^2)+(10^2-10)+(10-8) = 1000+900+90+2 = 1992$. A) 2008 B) 2002 C) 1998 D) 1992	5. D
6. $400 - 100 = 300$, and 300 is 50 less than 350. A) 350 B) 300 C) 200 D) 150	6. A
7. 5 nickels + 5 quarters = 25¢ + \$1.25 = \$1.50 = 15 dimes. A) 3 dimes B) 8 dimes C) 10 dimes D) 15 dimes	7. D
8. $7766-6677 = (7600-6600)+(100-77)+(66) = 1000+23+66 = 1089$. A) 1089 B) 1099 C) 1189 D) 1199	8. A
9. The five whole number divisors of 16 are: 1, 2, 4, 8, and 16. A) 16 B) 34 C) 85 D) 121	9. A
10. When I divided by 2, it was as if I had only doubled my age, added 10, then subtracted twice my age. This leaves 10. A) 0 B) 5 C) 10 D) 20	10. C
11. $31 + 29 = 60$; so, in a leap year, the 70th day will be March 10. A) 9th B) 10th C) 11th D) 12th	11. B
12. No prime larger than 6 can be a factor of $(1\times2\times3\times4\times5\times6)$. A) 7 B) 8 C) 9 D) 10	12. A
13. If *every* number is an 8, the average of *any* number of 8's is 8. A) 1 B) 8 C) 64 D) 88	13. B
14. Ten-million ÷ ten-thousand = $10\,000\,000 \div 10\,000 = 1000$. A) 10 B) 100 C) 1000 D) 10000	14. C
15. 475 min = 8 hrs−5 min; so 1 P.M. + 8 hrs−5 min = 8:55 P.M. A) 7:55 P.M. B) 8:45 P.M. C) 8:55 P.M. D) 9:55 P.M.	15. C

Go on to the next page ⫸ **6**

16. $2^8 - 2^7 - 2^6 - 2^5 = 256 - 128 - 64 - 32 = 256 - 224 = 32 = 2^5$. A) 2^5 B) 2^4 C) 2^3 D) 2^2	16. A
17. Mark is 12 and his sister is 6. Their mother is twice the sum of their ages, so their mother's age is $2(12 + 6) = 2(18) = 36$. A) 18 B) 24 C) 32 D) 36	17. D
18. It's a geometric fact: the sum of the angles of a triangle is 180°. A) 180° B) 120° C) 90° D) 60°	18. A
19. $7777 \div 7 = 1111$; $7777 \div 77 = 101$; $7777 \div 7777 = 1$. A) 7 B) 77 C) 777 D) 7777	19. C
20. 10% of 10% = 1/10 of 10% = 1%. If 1% is 2, then 100% is 200. A) 20 B) 100 C) 120 D) 200	20. D
21. If the shuttle circles the earth once every half-hour it circles the earth twice every hour, which is 48 times in 24 hours. A) 48 B) 36 C) 24 D) 12	21. A
22. Dividing 58 000 by 58, the quotient is 1000, with no remainder. Dividing 57 999 by 58, the quotient is 1 less than 1000; it's 999. A) 1 B) 9 C) 99 D) 999	22. D
23. The primes are 23 and 29, and their sum is $23 + 29 = 52$. A) 44 B) 50 C) 52 D) 54	23. C
24. $\sqrt{1} + \sqrt{4} + \sqrt{9} + \sqrt{16} = 1 + 2 + 3 + 4 = 10 = \sqrt{100}$. A) $\sqrt{10}$ B) $\sqrt{25}$ C) $\sqrt{30}$ D) $\sqrt{100}$	24. D
25. In a square, $p = 4s$, so a side is 1/4 (or 25%) of the perimeter. A) 4 B) 25 C) 40 D) 400	25. B
26. Any such whole number must have at least one digit different from 0. The sum of all of the digits of 100 or 1000 is 1. A) 0 B) 1 C) 2 D) 3	26. B
27. The choices other than 48 are not the *greatest* common factor. A) 4 B) 8 C) 12 D) 48	27. D
28. The *prime* factorization of 72 is $2 \times 2 \times 2 \times 3 \times 3 = 2^3 \times 3^2$. A) $2^2 \times 9$ B) $2^3 \times 9$ C) $2^3 \times 3^2$ D) $2^2 \times 3^2$	28. C
29. Sine $77 \times 888 = 7 \times 11 \times 8 \times 111$ and $88 \times 777 = 8 \times 11 \times 7 \times 111$, the $\blacklozenge$ can be replaced by =, since $(77 \times 888) = (88 \times 777)$. A) < B) = C) > D) ≠	29. B
30. $0 = 0 \times 1$, $2 = 1 \times 2$, and $56 = 7 \times 8$. Only $63 = 7 \times 9$ *cannot* be expressed as the product of two consecutive whole numbers. A) 0 B) 2 C) 56 D) 63	30. D

Go on to the next page ▶ **6**

31. Since each perimeter is 4, each side is 1. It would take 4 rows of 4 squares each, 16 in all, to cover the square with side 4. A) 1 B) 4 C) 8 D) 16	31. D
32. If the sum of five *different* positive integers is 500, the sum $1+2+3+4+490 = 500$ shows that the largest could be 490. A) 102 B) 490 C) 494 D) 499	32. B
33. Subtracting 6 from one of the numbers has the same effect as subtracting 1 from each of the six—so their average is 1 less. A) 6 B) 10 C) 11 D) 12	33. C
34. With 1992 numbers *all together*, the *number* of evens minus the *number* of odds must be even, so the difference cannot be 1111. Examples are $996-996=0$; $1346-646 = 700$; $1992-0 = 1992$. A) 0 B) 700 C) 1111 D) 1992	34. C
35. A hexagon has 6 sides. Since the length of each side is a whole number, the perimeter of the hexagon must be greater than 5. A) 5 B) 1991 C) 1992 D) 1993	35. A
36. $3-2 = 1, 5-3 = 2$, and $11-3 = 8$. The difference cannot be 7. A) 1 B) 2 C) 7 D) 8	36. C
37. A circle and a square intersect as shown. Since a side of the square is 2, its area is 4. The *full* circle's area is $\pi r^2 = 4\pi$, so the quarter-circle is π, and shaded $= 4-\pi$. A) $4\pi - 4$ B) $4 - \pi$ C) $2\pi - 4$ D) $\pi - 2$	37. B
38. The 2nd number exceeds the 1st by 4; the 3rd number exceeds the 1st by $4+4 = 2\times4$; the 4th number exceeds the 1st by $4+4+4 = 3\times4$. The 200th number exceeds the first by $199\times4 = 796$. A) 200 B) 796 C) 800 D) 804	38. B
39. The sum of the squares of the first 20 positive integers is 2870. The sum of the squares of the first 19 is $2870-20^2 = 2870-400$. A) 2350 B) 2361 C) 2470 D) 2850	39. C
40. My dog was 100 m from home, and my cat was 80 m from home. I called them, and they both ran directly home. If my dog ran twice as fast as my cat, my cat ran only 50 m when my dog ran 100 m; and the cat was $80-50 = 30$ m from home. A) 20 m B) 30 m C) 40 m D) 50 m	40. B

The end of the contest ✍🏻 **6**

Information & Solutions

Tuesday, March 9, 1993

Contest Information

6

- **Solutions** Turn the page for detailed contest solutions (written in the question boxes) and letter answers (written in the *Answers* column to the right of each question).

- **Scores** Please remember that *this is a contest, not a test*—and there is no "passing" or "failing" score. Few students score as high as 30 points (75% correct). Students with half that, 15 points, *deserve commendation!*

- **Answers & Rating Scale** Turn to page 149 for the letter answers to each question and the rating scale for this contest.

1. $900 + 90 + 9 + 1 = 999 + 1 = 1000$. A) 100 B) 991 C) 1000 D) 9000	1. C
2. 6 days ago was Tues. Today is Mon. In 8 days it will be Tues. A) Monday B) Tuesday C) Wednesday D) Thursday	2. B
3. $12345 + 123450 = 12345 \times 1 + 12345 \times 10 = 12345 \times 11$. A) 2 B) 10 C) 11 D) 22	3. C
4. There are 30 students in Pat's math class. With twice as many girls as boys, the class has 20 girls and 10 boys. A) 5 B) 8 C) 10 D) 20	4. C
5. $512 \times 2 = 1024 = 32 \times 32$. A) 4 B) 8 C) 16 D) 32	5. D
6. If the area is 24, the other side is 6, so the perimeter is $4 + 4 + 6 + 6 = 20$. 4 A) 10 B) 16 C) 20 D) 24	6. C
7. $(2 + 4 + 6 + 8 + 10) \div (10 + 8 + 6 + 4 + 2) = 30 \div 30 = 1$. A) 0 B) 1 C) 2 D) 60	7. B
8. Twice 7, plus 4 is 18, so 7 is my house number. A) 5 B) 7 C) 14 D) 40	8. B
9. $1+10 + 2+10 + 3+10 + 4+10 + 5+10 = 1+2+3+4+5 + 50$. A) 10 B) 50 C) 60 D) 65	9. B
10. (5 sides of a pentagon) + (4 sides of a trapezoid) − (6 sides of a hexagon) = 3 sides of a triangle. A) a triangle B) a square C) a pentagon D) an octagon	10. A
11. $99 \times 9 = (100-1) \times 9$. This is slightly less than 100×9, so it's D. A) $990 - 9$ B) $990 - 90$ C) $900 - 99$ D) $900 - 9$	11. D
12. If a side is 1, the perimeter is 4, for a 1:4 ratio. A) 2:1 B) 1:1 C) 1:2 D) 1:4	12. D
13. The primes less than 10 are 2, 3, 5, and 7. Their product is 210. A) 70 B) 60 C) 12 D) 4	13. A
14. $64 \div 2 = 32 = 2 \times 16$. A) 16 B) 32 C) 64 D) 128	14. A
15. $3^2 + 3^2 + 3^2 + 3^2 = 9 + 9 + 9 + 9 = 36 = 6^2$. A) 4^2 B) 6^2 C) 12^2 D) 33^2	15. B

Go on to the next page ⫸ **6**

16. The ten-thousands' digit plus the millions' digit of 1 234 567 890 is 6 + 4 = 10.

A) 7   B) 9   C) 10   D) 11

16. C

17. A cube has 4 top edges, 4 bottom edges, and 4 vertical edges.

A) 6   B) 8   C) 10   D) 12

17. D

18. A balloon ride can take *at most* 3 people at a time. If 41 people want to fly in the balloon, the least number of rides needed is 41 ÷ 3, rounded *up* to 14.

A) 12   B) 13   C) 14   D) 15

18. C

19. The average is the middle number, 5.

A) 5   B) 6   C) 9   D) 45

19. A

20. Ali, Barb, and Cal *were* all born on April 1, in *different* years. This coming Apr 1, if I add all their ages, I'll get 9. Since the youngest possible ages are 1 and 2, the oldest possible age is 6.

A) 7   B) 5   C) 3   D) 1

20. A

21. A triangle's longest side *is less than* the sum of the other two sides.

A) 0, 1, 2   B) 1, 2, 3   C) 2, 3, 4   D) 2, 4, 6

21. C

22. If a whole number is multiplied by itself, the ones' digit of the product could be 1 (1×1) or 5 (5×5) or 9 (3×3), but not 7.

A) 1   B) 5   C) 7   D) 9

22. C

23. The g.c.d. = the product of *all* common divisors = $3 \times 6 \times 9$.

A) 3   B) $3 \times 6 \times 9$ C) $30 \times 60 \times 90$ D) $10 \times 3 \times 6 \times 9$

23. B

24. The string 12 meters long is cut into 6 pieces of length 2 m. The sum of the lengths of any 4 of these pieces is 4×2 m = 8 m.

A) 2 m   B) 4 m   C) 6 m   D) 8 m

24. D

25. $49 = 7 \times 7$; $51 = 3 \times 17$. The first prime is 53.

A) 59   B) 57   C) 53   D) 51

25. C

26. $\sqrt{9 + 16 + 144} = \sqrt{169} = 13 = 3 + 4 + 6 = \sqrt{9} + \sqrt{16} + \sqrt{36}$.

A) $\sqrt{36}$ B) $\sqrt{100}$ C) $\sqrt{144}$ D) $\sqrt{169}$

26. A

27. Martha had $1.50. She bought 12 caramels at 5¢ each, spending 60¢ and leaving her with 90¢. With 90¢, she can buy 90 ÷ 10 = 9 mints at 10¢ each.

A) 12   B) 11   C) 10   D) 9

27. D

28. If 1000% is 100, then (1/10)th of that, 10, is 100% of the number.

A) 1   B) 10   C) 100   D) 1000

28. B

29. If 1 more than a 3-digit number is a 4-digit number, then the numbers are 999 and 1000 and their sum is 1999.

A) 1001   B) 1100   C) 1999   D) 2001

29. C

Go on to the next page ⟶ **6**

30. Jodie has just begun to read a 160-page book. If she reads 20 pages every day, she will finish the book in $160 \div 20 = 8$ days.

A) 8 days   B) 18 days   C) 20 days   D) 80 days

30.

A

31. Ten years ago, the sum of the ages of my mother and father was 71. Each has aged 10 years, so the sum of their ages is now 91.

A) 51   B) 61   C) 81   D) 91

31.

D

32. For the first 50 km, they drove at 50 km/hr—that took 1 hr. For the other second 50 km, they drove at 25 km/hr—that took 2 hrs. The trip took 3 hrs.

A) 3   B) 4   C) 5   D) 6

32.

A

33. Since $12 \times 166 + 1 = 1992 + 1 = 1993$, the month will be April.

A) January   B) February   C) March   D) April

33.

D

34. In weight, 45 mice = $3 \times (15$ mice$)$ = $3 \times (2$ cats$)$ = $2 \times (3$ cats$)$ = $2 \times (2$ dogs$)$ = 4 dogs.

A) 3   B) 4   C) 6   D) 9

34.

B

35. The sum of the digits of 1993 is $1+9+9+3$, or 22. At some time in the future, the sum of the digits of a year will be 33. Since $9+9+9 = 27$, this will *first* occur in 6999, the 70th century.

A) 21st   B) 60th   C) 70th   D) 80th

35.

C

36. The shaded area is twice the unshaded. The unshaded area is 12, so the shaded area is 24 and the area of *ABCD* is 36.

A) 36   B) 30   C) 24   D) 18

36.

A

37. It takes 3 hours for the *minute* hand to go around 3 times, so the time will be 2 P.M.

A) 11:03 A.M.   B) 11:30 A.M.   C) 1:00 P.M.   D) 2:00 P.M.

37.

D

38. The 100 even numbers that add up to 10 100 are 2, 4, . . ., 200. The sum we want is $2 + 4 + \ldots + 200 + 202 = 10\,100 + 202$.

A) 10 302   B) 10 202   C) 10 201   D) 10 102

38.

A

39. In March, there are 31 days. I earned $930 \div 31$, which is $30 each day. For all of 1992, I earned $366 \times \$30 = \$10980$.

A) $11 346   B) $11 315   C) $10 980   D) $10 950

39.

C

40. $497+498+499+500 = 1994$; $509+510+511+512 = 2042$; $511+512+513+514 = 2050$. (Divide by 4, and "start" near the quotient.)

A) 1994   B) 2042   C) 2050   D) 2060

40.

D

The end of the contest ✍ **6**

Information & Solutions

Tuesday, March 8, 1994

Contest Information

6

- **Solutions** Turn the page for detailed contest solutions (written in the question boxes) and letter answers (written in the *Answers* column to the right of each question).

- **Scores** Please remember that *this is a contest, not a test*—and there is no "passing" or "failing" score. Few students score as high as 30 points (75% correct). Students with half that, 15 points, *deserve commendation!*

- **Answers & Rating Scale** Turn to page 150 for the letter answers to each question and the rating scale for this contest.

125

1.	$51+49 + 51+49 + 51+49 + 51+49 = 100 + 100 + 100 + 100 = 400.$				1. B
	A) 104	B) 400	C) 440	D) 800	

2. If a mischievous bookworm eats one book every 5 minutes for one hour, it eats $60 \div 5 = 12$ books during this hour.

A) 60   B) 30   C) 24   D) 12

2. D

3. Since multiplication precedes addition, $1\times1 + 1\times0 = 1 + 0 = 1.$

A) 0   B) 1   C) 2   D) 3

3. B

4. The train comes to town every day at 6 A.M. Between 11 A.M. Tuesday and 11 P.M. Friday, it comes to town on Wednesday, Thursday, and Friday mornings.

A) 3   B) 4   C) 5   D) 6

4. A

5. The sum of ten 456's $= 10\times456 = 4560.$

A) 466   B) 4104   C) 4560   D) 5016

5. C

6. $999 - 9 = 990 = 10\times99 = 10\times9\times11$, so 12 is *not* a factor.

A) 9   B) 10   C) 11   D) 12

6. D

7. $5+10+15+20 + 1+1+1+1+1 = 5+10+15+20 + 5.$ Since every term is divisible by 5, the remainder is 0.

A) 0   B) 1   C) 2   D) 4

7. A

8. $6+5\times[4+3\times(2+1)] = 6+5\times[4+9] = 6+5\times13 = 6+65 = 71.$

A) 61   B) 71   C) 143   D) 231

8. B

9. Since the thousandth's digit is 4, round 0.9949 down to 0.99.

A) 0.99   B) 0.994   C) 0.995   D) 1.00

9. A

10. $(1\times10^3) + (99\times10) + (4\times1) = 1000 + 990 + 4 = 1994.$

A) 1904   B) 1994   C) 1995   D) 2904

10. B

11. In the word *lunchtime*, there are 3 vowels. Since there are 9 letters altogether, the ratio is $3:9 = 1:3.$

A) 3:10   B) 2:3   C) 1:2   D) 1:3

11. D

12. Since $2000 - 1245 = 755$, we know that $2000 - 755 = 1245.$

A) 865   B) 855   C) 765   D) 755

12. D

13. $(41\times42) - (42\times40) = (42\times41)-(42\times40) = 42\times(41-40) = 42.$

A) 40   B) 41   C) 42   D) 84

13. C

14. Pat's trip began on the morning of August 12, so Pat fished on August 12, 13, 14, 15, 16, 17, 18, 19, 20, 21, 22, 23, 24, and 25, a total of 14 days.

A) 12   B) 13   C) 14   D) 15

14. C

15. $(20 + 30) \div (2 + 3) = 50 \div 5 = 10$

A) 5   B) 10   C) 20   D) 55

15. B

Go on to the next page ⟹ **6**

16.	One million divided by one hundred = $1\,000\,000 \div 100 = 10\,000$. A) 100 B) 1000 C) 10 000 D) 100 000	16. C
17.	$(8 \times 1000) + (7 \times 100) + (6 \times 10) + (5 \times 1) = 8000 + 700 + 60 + 5 = 8765$. A) 26 000 B) 8765 C) 1136 D) 26	17. B
18.	Sue is 11 years old and her sister is 7 years old. In 15 years, Sue will be 26, her sister will be 22, and 26 + 22 = 48. A) 33 B) 44 C) 45 D) 48	18. D
19.	$11\,000 + 1100 + 110 + 11 = 11 \times (1000 + 100 + 10 + 1) = 11 \times 1111$ A) 1101 B) 1111 C) 1121 D) 1 010 101	19. B
20.	345 minutes is 15 minutes less than 6 hours, so time is 9:30 P.M. A) 7:30 P.M. B) 8:30 P.M. C) 9:30 P.M. D) 10:30 P.M.	20. C
21.	Seventy-seven 77's = $77 \times 77 = 7 \times 11 \times 7 \times 11 = 7 \times 7 \times 11 \times 11$. A) 7×7×11×11 B) 7×7×7×7 C) 7×11 D) 7777	21. A
22.	If the distance from *A* to *B* is 4, then the vertical height of rectangle *ABCD* is 2, and the perimeter of *ABCD* is 2+4+2+4 = 12. A) 10 B) 12 C) 14 D) 16	22. B
23.	Since 9 quarters = $9 \times 5 = 45$ nickels, Don still owes Joe 20 nickels = 1 dollar = 10 dimes. A) 10 dimes B) 2 quarters C) 2 dollars D) 25¢	23. A
24.	To be divisible by 15, a number must be divisible by 3 and by 5. A) 35×8 B) 36×9 C) 39×10 D) 40×11	24. C
25.	If I round 1315 to the nearest ten, I get 1320. Then, I multiply by 3 to get 3960. To the nearest hundred, this is 4000. A) 3900 B) 3945 C) 3960 D) 4000	25. D
26.	Using a calculator, 15:20 = 33:44 = 120:160 = 0.75. A) 13:14 B) 15:20 C) 33:44 D) 120:160	26. A
27.	$10000 - 1000 + 1000 - 100 + 100 - 10 + 10 - 1 = 10000 - 1 = 9999$. A) 999 B) 9000 C) 9999 D) 99 999	27. C
28.	The average of four 8's and four 16's is 12, the average of four 12's. A) 12's B) 24's C) 48's D) 96's	28. A
29.	$\frac{1}{3} + \frac{1}{2} + \frac{1}{3} + \frac{1}{2} + \frac{1}{3} = \frac{1}{3} + \frac{1}{3} + \frac{1}{3} + \frac{1}{2} + \frac{1}{2} = 1 + 1 = 2$. A) $\frac{1}{13}$ B) $\frac{5}{13}$ C) $\frac{5}{6}$ D) 2	29. D
30.	In a right triangle, the sum of the degree measures of the two smaller angles is 90°, the same as the measure of the right angle. A) 45% B) 50% C) 90% D) 100%	30. D

Go on to the next page ➠ **6**

31. Multiply the ones' digits: 9×4×9 has a one's digit of 4. A) 2 B) 4 C) 6 D) 8	31. B
32. If equal numbers of 3's, 5's, and 7's are added to get 105, there must be 105÷(3+5+7) = 105÷15 = 7 of each. A) 7 B) 10 C) 21 D) 71	32. A
33. On a 50-question test, Dave got 80% of the questions right, and Janet got 90% of them right. Dave got 40 correct and Janet got 45 correct, and 45–40 = 5. A) 1 B) 5 C) 10 D) 45	33. B
34. Mike needs 1302 bricks to build a brick barbecue. Mike has 1302÷3 = 434 groups of 3 bricks. Each group weighs 2 kg, and 434×2 = 868 kg. A) 217 B) 434 C) 651 D) 868	34. D
35. The 2000 odd numbers between 1000 and 5000 *cannot* be written as the sum of two odd numbers, since every such sum is even. A) 0 B) 1 C) 1999 D) 2000	35. D
36. Pat and Lee counted leaves on two plants. Pat's got a 1-digit number. Lee got a 3-digit number. If the difference of the numbers was 91, the numbers were 100 and 9, and the sum is 109. A) 100 B) 109 C) 191 D) 200	36. B
37. Every 6th number (83 of them) is divisible by 6. Every 24th number (20 of them) is divisible by 6 and 8, and 83–20 = 63. A) 83 B) 73 C) 63 D) 53	37. C
38. Square *ABCD* has a perimeter of 8. The circle inscribed in this square has a radius of 1. The area of this circle is $\pi(1)^2 = \pi$. A) π B) 2π C) 4π D) 16π	38. A
39. If 1×2×3×4×5×6×7×8×9×10×11×12×13×14×15 = 1 307 674 368 000, and we multiply each of these 15 numbers by 10, the new product will have an *additional* 15 zeroes, and 15+4 = 19. A) 15 B) 18 C) 19 D) 20	39. C
40. Since 8615 is divisible by 5, 8617 is divisible by 7, 8619 is divisible by 3, and the rest are even, #(8620) = #(8614). A) 0 B) 1 C) 2 D) 3	40. A

The end of the contest 6

Information & Solutions

Tuesday, March 14, 1995

Contest Information

6

- **Solutions** Turn the page for detailed contest solutions (written in the question boxes) and letter answers (written in the *Answers* column to the right of each question).

- **Scores** Please remember that *this is a contest, not a test*—and there is no "passing" or "failing" score. Few students score as high as 30 points (75% correct). Students with half that, 15 points, *deserve commendation!*

- **Answers & Rating Scale** Turn to page 151 for the letter answers to each question and the rating scale for this contest.

1. Dropping the four 0's, $1000 + 900 + 90 + 5 = 1995$. A) 1995 B) 19 950 C) 199 500 D) 1 995 000	1. A
2. Nine hundred less than one thousand one = $1001 - 900 = 101$. A) 99 B) 100 C) 101 D) 1901	2. C
3. By definition, a triangle with sides of equal length is *isosceles*. A) scalene B) isosceles C) right D) equilateral	3. B
4. This year, there were $11 \times 121 - 11 \times 11$ fewer turkeys eaten than last year. Using a calculator, $11 \times 121 - 11 \times 11 = 1210$. A) 120 B) 121 C) 1200 D) 1210	4. D
5. 200% of 50% equals $2 \times 1/2 = 1 = 100\%$. A) 1% B) 100% C) 250% D) 10 000%	5. B
6. $(1995+1994+1993)-(1992+1991+1990) = 3+3+3 = 1990 - 1981$. A) 1999 B) 1993 C) 1987 D) 1981	6. D
7. There's only *one* such prime divisible by 2 (and that is 2 itself). A) 0 B) 1 C) 2 D) 7	7. B
8. $1+4+1+8+1+12+1+16 = 4+8+12+16+4$, of which 4 is a factor. A) 0 B) 1 C) 2 D) 3	8. A
9. All the figures below consist of the same four squares of equal size. Figure A has perimeter 8; the others all have perimeter 10. A) B) C) D)	9. A
10. Since 999999 is not divisible by 2, their gcd is 1. A) 1 B) 2 C) 3 D) 9	10. A
11. That number must be $10100 - 1111 = 8989$. A) 8989 B) 9090 C) 9191 D) 11211	11. A
12. If you make sure you do multiplications before substractions, $4-0 \times 2-0 \times 1 = 4-0-0 = 4$. A) 0 B) 2 C) 4 D) 8	12. C
13. A polygon has straight line segments as sides. A) triangle B) rhombus C) pentagon D) circle	13. D
14. $111111 + \ldots + 111111 + 222222 = 111111 \times 7 = 777777$ A) 1 111 111 B) 333 333 C) 666 666 D) 777 777	14. D
15. Pat wrote a word in secret code. In this code, 26 was "A," 25 was "B," etc. In this code, the five numbers 19 26 11 11 2 stand for the letters H, A, P, P, and Y. A) RATTY B) HAPPY C) HOPPY D) DANNY	15. B

Go on to the next page ⇒ **6**

16. $10 \times 25 + 10 \times 5 + 10 \times 1 = \$2.50 + 50¢ + 10¢ = \$3.10 = 31$ dimes. A) 11 dimes B) 21 dimes C) 30 dimes D) 31 dimes	16. D
17. 3456 is closer to 3500 than it is to 3400. A) 3000 B) 3400 C) 3500 D) 3460	17. C
18. $10 \div 1 + 20 \div 2 + 30 \div 3 + 40 \div 4 = 40 = 200 \div 5.$ A) 200 B) 100 C) 40 D) 8	18. A
19. If the product of an even and an odd number is $840 = 2^3 \times 105$, then the largest possible value of the odd number is 105. A) 21 B) 35 C) 105 D) 420	19. C
20. The sum of the two largest primes less than 30 is $29 + 23 = 52.$ A) 48 B) 52 C) 56 D) 68	20. B
21. Do $\times$ and $\div$ first, *in order of appearance*. Then $2 \times 2 + 8 \div 8 = 5.$ A) 2 B) 3 C) 4 D) 5	21. D
22. A bakery lowered its price for cookies from 25¢ each to 20¢ each. For \$1, you get 1 more cookie; for \$4, you get 4 more cookies. A) 1 B) 4 C) 5 D) 20	22. B
23. 11:33 A.M. is 1 hour 27 minutes = 87 minutes before 1 P.M. A) 27 B) 87 C) 93 D) 97	23. B
24. The average of 7 whole numbers is 7, so their sum is $7 \times 7 = 49.$ If 6 numbers are 1, then the seventh number $= 49 - 6 = 43.$ A) 1 B) 7 C) 13 D) 43	24. D
25. $5 \times 5 \times 5 \times 2 \times 2 \times 2 \times 2 \times 2 = (2 \times 2) \times (5 \times 5 \times 5) \times (2 \times 2 \times 2) = 4 \times 125 \times 8.$ A) 125 B) 125×2 C) 125×4 D) 125×8	25. D
26. The area of the wall is $12 \times 15 = 180$, and the area of each square is $3 \times 3 = 9.$ Therefore, Bob can paint at most $180 \div 9 = 20$ squares. A) 9 B) 18 C) 20 D) 60	26. C
27. $19951995 \div 1995 = 10001.$ Now use the pattern. A) 1111 C) 1001001001 B) 1010101 D) 1000100010001	27. D
28. Twice as many fidgets as widgets means there are 4 widgets. A) 3 B) 4 C) 13 D) 16	28. B
29. An isosceles right triangle has angles 45°, 45°, and 90°. A) 10° B) 40° C) 45° D) 100°	29. C

Go on to the next page ⫸ **6**

30. To check for an odd quotient, divide *only* the last two digits by 2. A) 456 456 456 456 456 B) 678 678 678 678 678 C) 432 432 432 432 432 D) 876 876 876 876 876	30. B
31. As shown, *ABCD* is a square and *ADE* is an equilateral triangle. The degree-measure of angle *BAE* = 90° − 60° = 30°. A) 30° B) 45° C) 60° D) 90°	31. A
32. 1:¼ = 1 ÷ ¼ = 1×4 = 4 = 4:1. A) $\frac{1}{2}$:2 B) 11111:44444 C) 1:$\frac{1}{4}$ D) 10^6:(4×10^6)	32. C
33. The primes could be 2, 3, and 5, whose product, 30, is divisible by 1, 2, 3, 5, 6, 10, 15, and 30—8 different factors altogether. A) 3 B) 6 C) 8 D) 9	33. C
34. Each factor is 2. By pattern, the exponent is (1995−1)÷2 = 997. A) 2×996 B) 2×997 C) 2^{996} D) 2^{997}	34. D
35. Use any value for *r*, say *r* = 1. Then the area of *C* divided by the area of *S* is π×1^2 = π divided by 1^2 = 1. The quotient is π. A) π B) 2π C) 4π D) 4	35. A
36. The product is 36 = 2×2×3×3 = 1×1×2×2×3×3. The least possible value of the sum is 1+1+2+2+3+3 = 12. A) 8 B) 12 C) 14 D) 16	36. B
37. 83×6 = 498, so we end a *CIRCUS* cycle at the 498th letter. Thus, the 499th letter is *C* and the 500th letter is *I*. A) *R* B) *U* C) *C* D) *I*	37. D
38. Every digit used is odd, and there are 5 odd digits. At most, there are 5×5×5 = 125 different numbers on my list. A) 125 B) 150 C) 333 D) 450	38. A
39. Notice that 2^3 + 2^3 = 2^4 and 2^4 + 2^4 = 2^5. Now use the pattern. A) 2^{1001} B) 2^{2000} C) 4^{1000} D) 4^{2000}	39. A
40. I multiplied one whole number by 18. I multiplied a second whole number by 21. Both products have 3 as a factor, so when I add the two, the sum must still have 3 as a factor. A) 1996 B) 1997 C) 1998 D) 1999	40. C

The end of the contest **6**

Information & Solutions

Tuesday, March 12, 1996

Contest Information

6

- **Solutions** Turn the page for detailed contest solutions (written in the question boxes) and letter answers (written in the *Answers* column to the right of each question).

- **Scores** Please remember that *this is a contest, not a test*—and there is no "passing" or "failing" score. Few students score as high as 30 points (75% correct). Students with half that, 15 points, *deserve commendation!*

- **Answers & Rating Scale** Turn to page 152 for the letter answers to each question and the rating scale for this contest.

1. My friend and I average 64¢ each. Our total is $2 \times 64¢ = \$1.28$. A) 16¢　　　B) 32¢　　　C) 64¢　　　D) \$1.28	1. D
2. If I rode two dozen sheep, I rode $2 \times 12 = 24$ sheep. A) 20　B) 24　C) 40　D) 48	2. B
3. $56 = 2 \times 28 = 2 \times 2 \times 14 = 2 \times 2 \times 2 \times 7$. A) 2×28　　　B) $2 \times 2 \times 14$ C) $2 \times 4 \times 7$　　　D) $2 \times 2 \times 2 \times 7$	3. D
4. Recall: $10 \times 77\,777\,777\,777 = 777\,777\,777\,770$. A) 10　B) 7　C) 1　D) 0	4. A
5. Today is Tues, 28 days ago was Tues, and 3 days earlier was Sat. A) Friday　　　B) Saturday　　　C) Sunday　　　D) Monday	5. B
6. If each equilateral triangle shown has a perimeter of 6, each side is 2 and the figure's perimeter is 8. A) 6　　　B) 8　　　C) 10　　　D) 12	6. B
7. The remainders are: A) 2　B) 3　C) 4　D) 1. A) $7772 \div 7$　B) $6663 \div 6$　C) $5554 \div 5$　D) $4445 \div 4$	7. D
8. $444 + 333 + 222 + 111 - 999 = 111 \times (4+3+2+1-9) = 111 \times 1$. A) 1　　　B) 2　　　C) 3　　　D) 4	8. A
9. A trapezoid has *only one* pair of parallel sides. A) square　　　B) rectangle　　　C) trapezoid　　　D) rhombus	9. C
10. $1 \times 1 + 1 \times 9 + 1 \times 9 + 1 \times 6 = 1 + 9 + 9 + 6 = 25$. A) 25　　　B) 29　　　C) 1032　　　D) 1996	10. A
11. Since $60 - 57 = 3$ and $200 - 199 = 1$, Jan's original sum was too large by $3 + 1 = 4$. Jan must now subtract 4. A) 1　　　B) 2　　　C) 3　　　D) 4	11. D
12. $22 \times 10 + 22 \times 10^2 + 22 \times 10^3 = 22 \times (10+100+1000) = 22 \times 1110$. A) 22×10^5　B) 22×10^6　C) 22×1110　D) 22×1111	12. C
13. 1 can covers 5 m². To paint 4 walls, each 18 m² in area, I'd need $(4 \times 18)/5 = 14.4$ cans. Since 14 cans is not enough, buy 15 cans. A) 4　　　B) 7 C) 14　　　D) 15	13. D
14. $1 \times 9 \times 81 = 81 \times 9 = (3 \times 27) \times 9$. A) 1　B) 3　C) 9　D) 27	14. C
15. Twice as many sides as a triangle (3 sides) is a hexagon (6 sides). A) hexagon　　　B) pentagon　　　C) trapezoid　　　D) rhombus	15. A

Go on to the next page ▐▉▶ **6**

16. The Bush has twice as many berries each year as the previous year. Let's make a list: year 1 = 1; year 2 = 2; year 3 = 4; year 4 = 8; year 5 = 16; year 6 = 32; year 7 = 64; year 8 = 128. A) 7 years B) 8 years C) 49 years D) 50 years	16. B
17. My clock stopped running 5 hours 33 minutes after 2:27 P.M, which is 8 P.M. A) 5:00 P.M. B) 6:00 P.M. C) 7:00 P.M. D) 8:00 P.M.	17. D
18. $(1000 + 200 + 30 + 4) \times 9$, when simplified, has the same ones' digit as 4×9. A) 6 B) 7 C) 8 D) 9	18. A
19. 13 955 rounded to nearest: ten (13 960), hundred (14 000), thousand (14 000), and ten thousand (10 000). A) 10 000 B) 13 960 C) 13 900 D) 14 000	19. C
20. When each term is 1 more than a multiple of 4, the remainder is 1. A) 0 B) 1 C) 2 D) 3	20. B
21. For the ratio equivalent to $33 : 11 = 3 : 1$, see the work below. A) $(3 \div 3):(1 \div 1) = 1:1$ B) $(1+33):(1+11) = 34:12 = 17:6$ C) $(3 \times 3):(1 \times 1) = 9:1$ D) $(3 + 3):(1 + 1) = 6:2 = 3:1$	21. D
22. Look at the work below to see which is *not* a factor of $3 \times 5 \times 7$. A) $15 = 3 \times 5$ B) $21 = 3 \times 7$ C) $30 = 2 \times 3 \times 5$ D) $35 = 5 \times 7$	22. C
23. 12 coins, all nickels and dimes, are worth $1.00. Try 9 dimes and 3 nickels: too many dimes. Try 8 dimes and 4 nickels: it works. A) 2 B) 4 C) 6 D) 8	23. B
24. (A square) ÷ (the number being squared) always = (the number). A) 12345654321 B) 12345654321² C) 1 D) 2	24. A
25. If the frame of a ferris wheel is a circle with a 10 m diameter, the circumference of this circle = $\pi d = 10\pi$ m. A) 5π m B) 10π m C) 20π m D) 25π m	25. B
26. Of 30 students, 5 play both, 7 play only football, 12 play only soccer, and $30 - 5 - 7 - 12 = 6$ play neither. A) 1 B) 4 C) 6 D) 11	26. C
27. $50 \times 40 \times 30 \times 20 \times 10 = 5 \times 4 \times 3 \times 2 \times 1 \times 10^5$. A) 10 B) 50 C) 10 000 D) 100 000	27. D
28. The least common multiples are: A) 35 B) 15 C) 24 D) 18. A) 5 and 7 B) 3 and 15 C) 6 and 8 D) 6 and 9	28. A
29. For 28: $1+2+4+7+14+28 = 2 \times 28$. [Another *perfect* number is 6.] A) 8 B) 12 C) 24 D) 28	29. D

Go on to the next page ▌▌▌➡ **6**

30. If the lengths of the sides of the squares at the right are 2 and 4, the perimeter of the figure is 20. A) 18 B) 20 C) 22 D) 24		30. B

31. Pat has $30 to play miniature golf. If games are $4 each, or $8 for three, Pat can play 9 games for $3 \times \$8$ and Pat has $6 left, enough for 1 more game and $2 left over.

A) 7   B) 9   C) 10   D) 12

31. C

32. $\sqrt{4 \times 4} \times \sqrt{4 \times 4} = 4 \times 4 = 16.$

A) 4   B) 8   C) 16   D) 64

32. C

33. Maria is 160 cm tall. If she drinks a magic potion that makes her 20% of her height, her height will be 0.2×160 cm = 32 cm.

A) 8 cm   B) 32 cm   C) 128 cm   D) 3200 cm

33. B

34. In a camel herd with 80 legs, there are 20 camels, so 10 have one hump and 10 have two. The total number of humps is $10 \times 1 + 10 \times 2 = 30.$

A) 20   B) 30   C) 60   D) 120

34. B

35. There are 30 students in a class. There could be 6 groups of 2 boys and 3 girls, a 2:3 ratio.

A) 2:3   B) 3:5   C) 2:6   D) 3:4

35. A

36. $1000-1 + 1000-2 + 1000-3 + \ldots + 1000-99 + 1000-100$ is one hundred 1000's $- (1+2+ \ldots +99+100) = 100\,000 - 5050.$

A) 4050   B) 40\,050   C) 94\,950   D) 95\,950

36. C

37. There are 6 1×1's, 3 1×2's, 4 2×1's, 2 3×1's, 2 2×2's, and 1 3×2, for a total of 18 rectangles.

A) 15   B) 16   C) 17   D) 18

37. D

38. A grid is "checkerboarded" with alternating black and white squares. In the first 12 rows (156 squares), half (78) are black and half (78) are white. In the 13th row, 7 are black and 6 are white. Total: 85 black and 84 white.

A) $\frac{85}{169}$ B) $\frac{84}{169}$ C) $\frac{1}{2}$ D) $\frac{2}{3}$

38. A

39. Each small circle has diameter 6. The diameter of the large circle is 12. The shaded region is the large circle $-$ 2 small circles $= 36\pi - 2(9\pi) = 18\pi.$

A) 18π B) 27π C) 72π D) 108π

39. A

40. Each number on Lee's list must have the same remainder when divided by 7. Divide each choice by 7. The respective remainders are 2, 2, 2, and 4. Thus, 107, 184, and 534 work.

A) 107   B) 184   C) 534   D) 641

40. D

The end of the contest ✍ **6**

Answer Keys &
Difficulty Ratings

• • • • • • • • • • • • • • • • •

1991-92 through 1995-96

ANSWERS, 1991-92 4th Grade Contest

1. A	7. C	13. B	19. C	25. B
2. B	8. B	14. C	20. D	26. D
3. C	9. B	15. C	21. A	27. C
4. A	10. B	16. B	22. C	28. A
5. C	11. D	17. A	23. D	29. D
6. B	12. A	18. D	24. D	30. A

RATE YOURSELF!!!
for the 1991-92 4th GRADE CONTEST

Score	Rating
27-30	Another Einstein
24-26	Mathematical Wizard
22-23	School Champion
19-21	Grade Level Champion
17-18	Best In The Class
14-16	Excellent Student
11-13	Good Student
9-10	Average Student
0-8	Better Luck Next Time

ANSWERS, 1992-93 4th Grade Contest

1. C	7. A	13. B	19. C	25. B
2. B	8. B	14. D	20. C	26. D
3. A	9. C	15. A	21. A	27. D
4. B	10. D	16. B	22. D	28. C
5. B	11. A	17. C	23. A	29. C
6. D	12. C	18. A	24. A	30. D

RATE YOURSELF!!!
for the 1992-93 4th GRADE CONTEST

Score	Rating
27-30	Another Einstein
23-26	Mathematical Wizard
20-22	School Champion
18-19	Grade Level Champion
16-17	Best In The Class
14-15	Excellent Student
12-13	Good Student
9-11	Average Student
0-8	Better Luck Next Time

ANSWERS, 1993-94 4th Grade Contest

1. C	7. D	13. C	19. D	25. D
2. B	8. B	14. B	20. B	26. C
3. D	9. A	15. D	21. D	27. A
4. C	10. A	16. B	22. B	28. A
5. C	11. D	17. C	23. A	29. D
6. B	12. B	18. C	24. A	30. C

RATE YOURSELF!!!
for the 1993-94 4th GRADE CONTEST

Score	Rating
29-30	Another Einstein
26-28	Mathematical Wizard
24-25	School Champion
21-23	Grade Level Champion
19-20	Best In The Class
16-18	Excellent Student
14-15	Good Student
11-13	Average Student
0-10	Better Luck Next Time

ANSWERS, 1994-95 4th Grade Contest

1. C	7. D	13. B	19. B	25. C
2. C	8. B	14. C	20. C	26. D
3. B	9. B	15. C	21. A	27. B
4. A	10. A	16. A	22. D	28. D
5. D	11. D	17. C	23. A	29. B
6. C	12. C	18. B	24. B	30. D

RATE YOURSELF!!!
for the 1994-95 4th GRADE CONTEST

Score	Rating
28-30	Another Einstein
25-27	Mathematical Wizard
23-24	School Champion
20-22	Grade Level Champion
17-19	Best In The Class
15-16	Excellent Student
12-14	Good Student
10-11	Average Student
0-9	Better Luck Next Time

ANSWERS, 1995-96 4th Grade Contest

1. A	7. D	13. B	19. C	25. D
2. D	8. D	14. D	20. C	26. C
3. B	9. C	15. A	21. D	27. A
4. A	10. A	16. B	22. C	28. B
5. C	11. D	17. A	23. B	29. A
6. B	12. C	18. B	24. B	30. C

RATE YOURSELF!!!
for the 1995-96 4th GRADE CONTEST

Score	Rating
27-30	Another Einstein
25-26	Mathematical Wizard
22-24	School Champion
20-21	Grade Level Champion
17-19	Best In The Class
15-16	Excellent Student
12-14	Good Student
9-11	Average Student
0-8	Better Luck Next Time

ANSWERS, 1991-92 5th Grade Contest

1. A	7. B	13. A	19. C	25. D
2. B	8. D	14. B	20. D	26. B
3. B	9. A	15. C	21. C	27. D
4. D	10. C	16. D	22. C	28. C
5. B	11. B	17. B	23. A	29. D
6. C	12. D	18. A	24. A	30. B

RATE YOURSELF!!!
for the 1991-92 5th GRADE CONTEST

Score		Rating
27-30		Another Einstein
25-26		Mathematical Wizard
22-24		School Champion
20-21		Grade Level Champion
17-19		Best In The Class
15-16		Excellent Student
13-14		Good Student
10-12		Average Student
0-9		Better Luck Next Time

ANSWERS, 1992-93 5th Grade Contest

1. C	7. B	13. C	19. A	25. B
2. D	8. C	14. B	20. D	26. D
3. B	9. A	15. C	21. C	27. A
4. B	10. A	16. A	22. B	28. D
5. C	11. D	17. D	23. A	29. D
6. B	12. C	18. A	24. C	30. B

RATE YOURSELF!!!
for the 1992-93 5th GRADE CONTEST

Score		Rating
28-30		Another Einstein
25-27		Mathematical Wizard
22-24		School Champion
20-21		Grade Level Champion
17-19		Best In The Class
14-16		Excellent Student
12-13		Good Student
8-11		Average Student
0-7		Better Luck Next Time

144

ANSWERS, 1993-94 5th Grade Contest

1. B	7. C	13. C	19. A	25. B
2. B	8. D	14. C	20. C	26. A
3. A	9. B	15. D	21. D	27. B
4. B	10. D	16. A	22. C	28. A
5. A	11. C	17. B	23. D	29. C
6. A	12. C	18. D	24. B	30. B

RATE YOURSELF!!!
for the 1993-94 5th GRADE CONTEST

Score	Rating
27-30	Another Einstein
25-26	Mathematical Wizard
22-24	School Champion
19-21	Grade Level Champion
16-18	Best In The Class
13-15	Excellent Student
11-12	Good Student
9-10	Average Student
0-8	Better Luck Next Time

ANSWERS, 1994-95 5th Grade Contest

1. D	7. D	13. A	19. B	25. C
2. D	8. A	14. A	20. C	26. D
3. A	9. C	15. D	21. D	27. B
4. C	10. C	16. B	22. B	28. D
5. D	11. B	17. C	23. D	29. A
6. A	12. B	18. C	24. A	30. C

RATE YOURSELF!!!
for the 1994-95 5th GRADE CONTEST

Score	Rating
28-30	Another Einstein
25-27	Mathematical Wizard
23-24	School Champion
20-22	Grade Level Champion
17-19	Best In The Class
15-16	Excellent Student
13-14	Good Student
10-12	Average Student
0-9	Better Luck Next Time

ANSWERS, 1995-96 5th Grade Contest

1. C	7. A	13. B	19. A	25. D
2. D	8. D	14. B	20. D	26. C
3. D	9. C	15. D	21. A	27. A
4. B	10. A	16. C	22. D	28. C
5. B	11. C	17. D	23. C	29. B
6. A	12. C	18. A	24. B	30. B

RATE YOURSELF!!!
for the 1995-96 5th GRADE CONTEST

Score	Rating
28-30	Another Einstein
25-27	Mathematical Wizard
22-24	School Champion
20-21	Grade Level Champion
17-19	Best In The Class
15-16	Excellent Student
12-14	Good Student
10-11	Average Student
0-9	Better Luck Next Time

ANSWERS, 1991-92 6th Grade Contest

1. D	9. A	17. D	25. B	33. C
2. B	10. C	18. A	26. B	34. C
3. C	11. B	19. C	27. D	35. A
4. A	12. A	20. D	28. C	36. C
5. D	13. B	21. A	29. B	37. B
6. A	14. C	22. D	30. D	38. B
7. D	15. C	23. C	31. D	39. C
8. A	16. A	24. D	32. B	40. B

RATE YOURSELF!!!
for the 1991-92 6th GRADE CONTEST

Score	Rating
37-40	Another Einstein
34-36	Mathematical Wizard
30-33	School Champion
26-29	Grade Level Champion
24-25	Best In The Class
20-23	Excellent Student
17-19	Good Student
13-16	Average Student
0-12	Better Luck Next Time

ANSWERS, 1992-93 6th Grade Contest

1. C	9. B	17. D	25. C	33. D
2. B	10. A	18. C	26. A	34. B
3. C	11. D	19. A	27. D	35. C
4. C	12. D	20. A	28. B	36. A
5. D	13. A	21. C	29. C	37. D
6. C	14. A	22. C	30. A	38. A
7. B	15. B	23. B	31. D	39. C
8. B	16. C	24. D	32. A	40. D

RATE YOURSELF!!!
for the 1992-93 6th GRADE CONTEST

Score	Rating
38-40	Another Einstein
35-37	Mathematical Wizard
31-34	School Champion
27-30	Grade Level Champion
25-26	Best In The Class
22-24	Excellent Student
18-21	Good Student
14-17	Average Student
0-13	Better Luck Next Time

ANSWERS, 1993-94 6th Grade Contest

1. B	9. A	17. B	25. D	33. B
2. D	10. B	18. D	26. A	34. D
3. B	11. D	19. B	27. C	35. D
4. A	12. D	20. C	28. A	36. B
5. C	13. C	21. A	29. D	37. C
6. D	14. C	22. B	30. D	38. A
7. A	15. B	23. A	31. B	39. C
8. B	16. C	24. C	32. A	40. A

RATE YOURSELF!!!
for the 1993-94 6th GRADE CONTEST

Score	Rating
38-40	Another Einstein
36-37	Mathematical Wizard
32-35	School Champion
29-31	Grade Level Champion
25-28	Best In The Class
21-24	Excellent Student
17-20	Good Student
13-16	Average Student
0-12	Better Luck Next Time

ANSWERS, 1994-95 6th Grade Contest

1. A	9. A	17. C	25. D	33. C
2. C	10. A	18. A	26. C	34. D
3. B	11. A	19. C	27. D	35. A
4. D	12. C	20. B	28. B	36. B
5. B	13. D	21. D	29. C	37. D
6. D	14. D	22. B	30. B	38. A
7. B	15. B	23. B	31. A	39. A
8. A	16. D	24. D	32. C	40. C

RATE YOURSELF!!!
for the 1994-95 6th GRADE CONTEST

Score	Rating
37-40	Another Einstein
34-36	Mathematical Wizard
30-33	School Champion
26-29	Grade Level Champion
24-25	Best In The Class
20-23	Excellent Student
16-19	Good Student
12-15	Average Student
0-11	Better Luck Next Time

ANSWERS, 1995-96 6th Grade Contest

1. D	9. C	17. D	25. B	33. B
2. B	10. A	18. A	26. C	34. B
3. D	11. D	19. C	27. D	35. A
4. A	12. C	20. B	28. A	36. C
5. B	13. D	21. D	29. D	37. D
6. B	14. C	22. C	30. B	38. A
7. D	15. A	23. B	31. C	39. A
8. A	16. B	24. A	32. C	40. D

RATE YOURSELF!!!
for the 1995-96 6th GRADE CONTEST

Score	Rating
38-40	Another Einstein
35-37	Mathematical Wizard
31-34	School Champion
28-30	Grade Level Champion
24-27	Best In The Class
21-23	Excellent Student
17-20	Good Student
13-16	Average Student
0-12	Better Luck Next Time

Math League Contest Books

4th Grade Through High School Levels

Written by Steven R. Conrad and Daniel Flegler, recipients of President Reagan's 1985 Presidential Awards for Excellence in Mathematics Teaching, each book provides schools and students with:

- Easy-to-use format designed for a 30-minute period
- Problems ranging from straightforward to challenging
- Contests from 4th grade through high school

1-10 copies of any one book: $12.95 each ($16.95 Canadian)
11 or more copies of any one book: $9.95 each ($12.95 Canadian)

Use the form below (or a copy) to order your books

Name: _____

Address: _____

City: _____ State: _____ Zip: _____
                        (or Province)   (or Postal Code)

Available Titles	**# of Copies**	**Cost**
Math Contests—Grades 4, 5, 6		
Volume 1: 1979-80 through 1985-86	_____	_____
Volume 2: 1986-87 through 1990-91	_____	_____
Volume 3: 1991-92 through 1995-96	_____	_____
Math Contests—Grades 7 & 8		
Volume 1: 1977-78 through 1981-82	_____	_____
Volume 2: 1982-83 through 1990-91	_____	_____
Math Contests—7, 8, & Algebra Course 1		
Volume 3: 1991-92 through 1995-96	_____	_____
Math Contests—High School		
Volume 1: 1977-78 through 1981-82	_____	_____
Volume 2: 1982-83 through 1990-91	_____	_____
Volume 3: 1991-92 through 1995-96	_____	_____
Shipping and Handling		$3.00

Please allow 4-6 weeks for delivery   Total: $_____

□ Check or Purchase Order Enclosed; **or**

□ Visa / MasterCard # _____

□ Exp. Date_____ Signature _____

Mail your order with payment to:
Math League Press
P.O. Box 720
Tenafly, NJ USA 07670

Phone: (201) 568-6328 • Fax: (201) 816-0125